War in Heaven

To my wonderful friends,
Tom + Gillian

[signature]

War in Heaven

The Arms Race in Outer Space

Helen Caldicott
and Craig Eisendrath

THE NEW PRESS

NEW YORK
LONDON

Requests for permission to reproduce selections from this book should be mailed to:
Permissions Department, The New Press, 38 Greene Street, New York, NY 10013.

Published in the United States by The New Press, New York, 2007
Distributed by W. W. Norton & Company, Inc., New York

LIBRARY OF CONGRESS CATALOGING-IN-PUBLICATION DATA

Caldicott, Helen.
    War in heaven : the arms race in outer space / Helen Caldicott and Craig Eisendrath.
        p. cm.
    Includes bibliographical references and index.
    ISBN: 978-1-59558-114-3 (hc.)
    1. Space weapons. 2. Space warfare. 3. Arms control. 4. Arms race—History—
21st century. I. Eisendrath, Craig R. II. Treaty on Principles Governing the Activities
of States in the Exploration and Use of Outer Space, Including the Moon and Other
Celestial Bodies (1967) III. Title.

UG1520.C35 2007
327.1'74—dc22   2006030551

The New Press was established in 1990 as a not-for-profit alternative to the large,
commercial publishing houses currently dominating the book publishing industry.
The New Press operates in the public interest rather than for private gain, and is committed
to publishing, in innovative ways, works of educational, cultural, and community value
that are often deemed insufficiently profitable.

www.thenewpress.com

A Caravan book.
For more information, visit www.caravanbooks.org.

Composition by Westchester Book Composition
This book was set in Bembo

Printed in the United States of America

10 9 8 7 6 5 4 3 2 1

Contents

Authors' Notes

In December of 1957, I was a private first-class in the U.S. Army stationed at Schofield Barracks in Hawaii. We had a Russian kid in our unit, and when we weren't on guard duty or peeling potatoes, he would translate programs for us from Radio Moscow. Right before Christmas, we heard a narrator telling a story to some children. He said, "Aloysha, look up in the sky. There are three moons, and two of them are Russian."

We were in the space age! The Russians had just put up their first sputniks, preempting the Americans much to their acute dismay. The Americans, not to be outdone, launched their own satellites early in 1958, although they were not as large or impressive as the Russians', but the space race had begun.

In May, released from the Army, and having passed all my exams and my security check, I entered the U.S. Foreign Service to begin my career as a diplomat. My first assignment was with the United Nations Political Office of the State Department in Washington. The subject of my assignment: the international control of outer space.

It was an exciting time. The United States and the Soviet Union had just begun to explore this new world, which began where satellites could orbit around the earth and then extended to the farthest reaches of the universe. It was a time that could be compared to another era, when a Spanish explorer, Christopher Columbus, had discovered that our planet was not flat, but across its oceans existed a new world.

What would follow? Would the nations of the world do what they did after 1492: arm themselves to the teeth, and carve up this new world into colonies and empires? Would we see the Americans and Soviets in a mad rush to claim their very own planets and various sections of space; and would other powers make similar claims? Would the great powers begin to fight wars in outer space?

Today, as the United States moves to weaponize outer space, I am asking the same questions I asked fifty years ago: will we arm outer space, as we have armed the land, and seas, and airspace? Are we heading toward wars in this new area? This book is an attempt to frame the moral and political issues that these questions raise: will arming outer space increase the world's security; do we need to weaponize outer space? In the end we argue that weaponizing outer space will make the world far more dangerous than it is now. We will be far less secure with space weapons than without them, because arming outer space will assuredly start an arms race in space, and possibly provoke a dreadful war. If we are to avoid this "star wars" we must act now. Let us not arm the heavens but keep them for peaceful purposes and for the solace and wonder which they have always provided.

—Craig Eisendrath

In 1999, I was invited by Bruce Gagnon, an Air Force pilot and former Republican, to attend a meeting in Florida that addressed the weaponization of space. Having never heard of this concept before and believing that the Cold War was over, I accepted the invitation with alacrity.

This meeting, which featured extremely knowledgeable people, made me realize that I had been living in a fool's paradise. To my horror I found that seventy-five military industrial corporations such as Lockheed Martin, Boeing, Raytheon, TRW Aerojet, Hughes Space, Sparta Corp, and Vista Technologies had produced a Long Range Plan, written with the cooperation of the U.S. Space Command, announcing a declaration of U.S. space leadership and calling for the funding of defensive systems and a "seamlessly integrated force of theater land, sea, air, and space capabilities through a worldwide global defense information network."

The U.S. Space Command would also "hold at risk" a finite number of "high value" earth targets with near instantaneous force application—the ability to kill from space.

As retired general Robert R. Fogelman, former Chief of Staff of the Air Force and a member of the Joint Chiefs of Staff, said, "I think that space, in and of itself, is going to be very quickly recognized as a fourth dimension of warfare."

I also discovered that the much-vaunted missile defense system was to be closely integrated with the weaponization of space and that all of the hardware and software would be made by the same firms, at the combined cost of hundreds of billions of dollars to the U.S. taxpayers. I staggered home from that meeting, deciding that I must become re-involved in educating the public about the impending catastrophe associated with the mad plans of the U.S. Space Command and its associated corporations.

—Helen Caldicott

Preface

If the stars should appear one night in a thousand years, how would men believe and adore; and reserve for many generations the remembrance of the city of God which had been shown!
—"Nature," by Ralph Waldo Emerson, 1836

It's politically sensitive, but it's going to happen. Some people don't want to hear this and it sure isn't in vogue, but—absolutely—we're going to fight in space. We're going to fight from space and we're going to fight into space. That's why the U.S. has developed programs in directed energy and hit-to-kill mechanisms. We will engage terrestrial targets someday— ships, airplanes, land targets—from space. We will engage targets in space, from space.
—William R. Scott, "USSC Prepares for Future Combat Missions in Space," *Aviation Week & Space Technology*, August 5, 1996

The Cold War is over, but many of us can remember the terror of living in that era. Tens of thousands of rockets were poised to strike the United States and the Soviet Union in less than an hour—all armed with hydrogen bombs hundreds of times stronger than the bombs that had leveled Hiroshima and Nagasaki. If war broke out, our countries would be seething wastes of radioactivity. Almost nothing would survive.

The Cold War began in 1945, immediately after World War II, and by 1958, both the United States and Russia had obtained hydrogen bombs of unbelievable destructive power. At the same time, both countries were developing intercontinental ballistic missiles (ICBMs) to speed the delivery of these satanic weapons to their targeted cities. Between them, the United States and the Soviet Union soon had the capacity to destroy the planet in a series of lightning strikes. During the 1960s, reports from the Rand Corporation, a national security research institution, predicted between one and two hundred million dead in the first nuclear exchange. Not only would millions die, but the planet would be permanently polluted with radioactivity. Nikita Khrushchev, the leader of the Soviet Union, said "Will the living envy the dead?"

The fact that the ICBMs were designed to exit the earth's atmosphere before raining death and destruction down on Moscow, St. Petersburg, New York, and Washington, marked the first instance of the use of outer space for military purposes. And once this threshold had been crossed, military planners realized that space itself could be militarized—satellites could be used to identify military targets on the other side of the world and accurately guide missiles to their targets. Before satellites were used in this way, it had not been feasible for the United States or the Soviet Union to fly over each others' territory under international law. The United States could not observe the Soviets, who might be developing a missile launching platform in some obscure area of Siberia, unless the United States overflew Soviet territory, a violation of national air space under international law and an act of war. Satellites allowed such observations to be made unobtrusively and legally for the purpose of either identifying targets or monitoring arms control agreements. This technology became even more important after the U-2 incident in 1960, when the American airplane pilot, Francis Gary Powers, was shot down while spying on the Soviet Union in a high altitude plane.

The military planners had still other ideas for the military uses of outer space. Not only could missiles move through outer space, and satellites spot targets and guide missiles, but weapons could be permanently placed in orbit outside the earth's atmosphere, and then, on a signal from the earth, bombard bases and cities. Bombardment satellites, and satellites to knock out the satellites of other countries, looked like the weapons of future wars.

At the same time that military planners were dreaming of space wars, others were imagining a wide range of ways by which space could be used to benefit humankind. First on the seas, and then in the air, human beings had expanded their horizons, and had begun to create a unified planet. Outer space held the exciting promise of a further extension of the human endeavor—a new frontier with the potential to benefit the entire species.

Scientific exploration held perhaps the greatest and most wonderful promise. Before satellite technology became available, the examination of the solar system, our own galaxy, and the universe was limited to rather primitive observations made from the ground, because telescopic sightings were restricted by the fog of the atmosphere, which seriously compromised their clarity. Observations from satellites, by contrast, transcended the atmosphere, which opened up a whole new field of scientific endeavor. For the first time we could observe the farther reaches of our planetary system with accuracy, and begin to understand the composition of our galaxy, and then of the universe as a whole. We began to comprehend the immensity of the universe that we inhabit—one hundred billion galaxies—and to be able to speculate on the world's origins based on the direct evidence provided by satellite observations. The earthly restrictions on scientific research that limited findings in the nineteenth century and earlier decades of the twentieth century were astonishingly superseded by the birth of a totally new field of astrophysics.

Outer space could also be used to establish a global communication system free from expensive and sometimes impracticable ground wires and cables. A small village in Nigeria, which previously had no communication with the rest of the world, could suddenly be linked via satellite, and people in this small village could speak with anyone in the world at relatively low cost.

Outer space could also be used to track worldwide weather, thereby creating an accurate system of weather prediction. Before space-based satellites, weather tracking and predictions had been sketchy at best, relying solely on ground observation and sightings from ships and planes, with great geographic areas of the planet left unreported. Now, satellites could record developments all over the earth. This comprehensive forecasting would be of immense advantage to people ranging from farmers, to pilots, travelers, and government planners.

Still another exciting possibility presented itself: any person on earth could be located immediately by satellite, whether driving a car down an unfamiliar highway, steering a ship in the ocean, or flying a plane. It was now impossible to get lost. A quick communication with the satellite system would give one exact coordinates, and if one were sick or injured, the chance of rescue. Satellites were now the means by which ships and planes could navigate with assurance around the world.

Information technology loomed in the future, and outer space technology would be an important part of that revolution. The science of artificial intelligence, which was begun in the 1930s and would provide the basis for the development of computers, was in rapid progress by the 1950s. Prophets could imagine a world in which all global information could be stored or transmitted, with outer space as the ideal venue for transmission—not only verbal communications could be exchanged, but industrial designs, patent information, and scientific data. All the world's store of information could be contained in computers, and transmitted as needed through the medium of outer space.

Parts of the earth that had never been photographed could now be mapped; conferences could now be achieved without the need for face-to-face communication, and virtual chat groups could be set up around the globe; radio and television broadcasts could now reach any part of the world; and worldwide systems of information, including the flight paths of planes, and the spread of epidemics, could be monitored. For the first time, the world could be united by information, although as globalization increased, many people became uneasy. Would this global integration homogenize and destroy cultures and subjugate economies before the gigantic, all-powerful multilateral corporations? Or, on the other hand, would it create a global consciousness and a more efficient production and flow of goods?

At the very beginning of the space age, humans asked: Would outer space be dominated by one powerful nation and weaponized, or would it become the common property of mankind? Outer space would either be a model for international cooperation or a venue for intense and destructive nationalism. Would it be the venue for wars and synchronized killings, or the common space for a complex of cooperative peaceful efforts benefiting our species? The two uses of outer space could not exist side by side. Space wars would destroy peaceful satellites and the international cooperation upon which the peaceful uses of outer space depend. Cooperation of this magnitude requires not only the absence of conflict, but the creation of international agreements on rules, for example, allocating the orbits in outer space to be used by satellites, and allocating specific parts of the radio frequency band for satellite communication.

It is at this point in 1958, at the dawn of the space age, that our story begins. This book starts by chronicling the series of good and bad decisions that have been made over a period of almost fifty years on a relatively ad hoc basis about how outer space will be used. It takes us up to the first decade of the twenty-first century, to a planet enriched with a world communication system, global meteorological forecasting, global exchange of information, a global positioning system, the wonders of outer space exploration, and the use of outer space to monitor arms control treaties. But it is also a world armed with nuclear intercontinental ballistic missiles (ICBMs) on hair-trigger alert, with an embryonic but extremely destabilizing missile defense system, and ten nations possessing dedicated military satellites to identify targets and to guide missiles.

On August 31, 2006, President Bush authorized a new national space policy. It differs significantly from the policy proclaimed ten years ago by President Clinton. Where the earlier document emphasized the peaceful uses of outer space, this document focuses on its military uses and aggressively proclaims its resistance to any attempt to infringe upon U.S. dominance or limit U.S. activity by international agreement. It states that the United States will "develop and deploy space capabilities that sustain U.S. advantage and support defense and intelligence transformation." It calls upon the Secretary of Defense to "maintain the capabilities to execute the space support, force enhancement, space control, and force application missions." It also states, "The United States will oppose the development of new legal regimes or other restrictions that seek to prohibit or limit U.S. access to or use of outer space. Proposed arms control agreements or restrictions must not impair the rights of the United States to conduct research, development, testing, and operations or other activities in space for U.S. national interests."[1]

The new national space policy lays the basis for a radical change of U.S. policy toward outer space—the deployment of weapons. After decades of research and development in outer space, we will show that the U.S. government is contemplating such deployment. Human beings find themselves at a major crossroads. The Unites States and other countries have a wide range of exceedingly dangerous weapons on the drawing board. If deployed, these weapons—designed specifically to bombard the earth and destroy satellites—could transform outer space into a major battleground, creating an arms race costing trillions of dollars, and, in a worst-case scenario, triggering a catastrophic nuclear war. This book looks at how the United States has progressed to the brink of this decision. It offers the first comprehensive overview, for the general reader, of the specific weapons being contemplated and developed. It argues that the first deployment would be disastrous for the human race, and explores the impact of deployment and the likely political, military, and environmental outcomes. Finally, it explores available means for avoiding such a catastrophe.

On May 16 and 17, 2005, the Nuclear Policy Research Institute, founded by Helen Caldicott, sponsored a major conference called "Full Spectrum Dominance," near Washington, D.C., inviting the country's leading experts on space weaponization and national missile defense to discuss the pros and cons of using outer space as a new battlefield. The conference was also attended by representatives from key countries in the field, including Russia, China, and Canada, as well as journalists representing important elements of the United States' print and electronic media. The papers at the conference presented up-to-date analyses by well-known insiders in the field. This book draws heavily on these papers (with the consent of the authors), and on the newspaper and journal articles that followed the conference.

The weaponization of outer space, currently buried under obscure categories in the Pentagon budget, is at the forefront of the Bush administration's agenda, and must be at the forefront of the national agenda.

On September 14, 2005, at a conference on space security, Congresswoman Loretta Sanchez (D-CA) put the issue succinctly:

> The U.S. space policy has global repercussions and a global dialogue is needed. Also, it is important for the American people to debate this issue. I believe this administration is pushing for the weaponization of space and I find the trend

disturbing for several reasons: 1) The Congress has not had a real dialogue and the American people do not understand what is happening; 2) the weaponization of space actually makes us less safe. I would prefer we put our resources elsewhere and that other nations would also like to put their resources elsewhere—such as to eliminate poverty. If the U.S. begins to put weapons in space I believe other nations will feel the need to close the gap and level the playing field. By attempting to create and maintain dominance in space, we are creating a new battlefield, and money that the U.S. is not in a position to spend (we have a $7.5 trillion dollar national debt), *will* be spent. . . . I think we can protect the interests of America and its allies without opening up the "Pandora's Box" of space weapons, nor do I believe that weaponizing space is inevitable.[2]

In a democracy, power lies with an informed and energized public who can compel their political representatives to make the world safe for them and their children. This book aims to inform the public of the immense dangers posed by the weaponization of outer space. It seeks to galvanize public opinion to stop space weaponization and promote outer space for what it can be: a venue for human cooperation and benefit. We must act today if we are to avoid a war in heaven tomorrow.

Acknowledgments

The authors would like to extend their thanks and appreciation to the speakers at the Full Spectrum Dominance Conference organized by the Nuclear Policy Research Institute in May 2005. They are listed here in alphabetical order: Ambassador Jonathan Dean, Dr. Everett Carl Dolman, Bruce Gagnon, Nancy Gallagher, Dr. Richard L. Garwin, Ambassador Thomas Graham, Laura Grego, William Hartung, Theresa Hitchens, General Charles Horner, John Isaacs, Jeffrey Lewis, Dr. Donald Louria, Mike Moore, Dr. John Polanyi, Dr. Theodore Postol, Dr. Steven Weinberg, Loring Wirbel, Dr. David Wright, Vladimir Yermakov, and Dr. Hui Zhang.

The authors also extend their gratitude to the following people who reviewed the manuscript in earlier drafts: Loring Wirbel, Theresa Hitchens, Bruce Gagnon, Ambassador Thomas Graham, Ambassador Jonathan Dean, Dr. Donald Louria, Joe Bock, and Cynda Collins-Arsenault. Their thoughtful comments and feedback were essential.

Our fine editor, Diane Wachtell, provided valuable feedback and guidance throughout the manuscript preparation.

Above all the authors acknowledge the invaluable assistance and guidance of Julie Enszer, without whom this book would not have been written.

All errors and inaccuracies are of course the authors' own.

War in Heaven

1

A Brief History of Outer Space

When I heard the learn'd astronomer;
When the proofs, the figures, were ranged in columns
  before me;
When I was shown the charts and diagrams, to add, di-
  vide, and measure them;
When I, sitting, heard the astronomer where he lec-
  tured with much applause in the lecture-room,
How soon unaccountable, I became tired and sick,
Till rising and gliding out, I wander'd off by myself,
In the mystical moist night-air, and from time to time,
Look'd up in perfect silence at the stars.
                                      —Walt Whitman

The threat ladies and gentlemen I believe is real. It's a
threat to our economic well-being. This is why we must
work together to find common ground between com-
mercial imperatives and the President's tasking me for
space control and protection.
          —"Implementing Our Vision for Space Control,"
      Speech by General Richard B. Meyers, United States Space
                              Foundation, Colorado Springs,
                                              April 7, 1999[1]

On January 31, 1958, shortly after the Soviet Union launched
Sputnik 1, the chief of staff of the air force, Thomas Dresser White,
outlined a new policy in response to the Soviet challenge at an address to the National Press Club in Washington. The Soviet Union,
he said, had one-upped the United States. For the first time since
1814, the U.S. homeland was in mortal danger; no longer would

3

the Atlantic and Pacific moats protect it. America's answer to the Soviet challenge would require the military use of space. "I feel in the future," White said, "whoever has the capability to control space will likewise possess the capability to exert control of the surface of the earth." The United States answered the Russians with Explorer I, which, although smaller than Sputnik, at least put the United States back in what suddenly had become the "space race." While on the surface the rivalry was about nonmilitary exploits in space, both Americans and Russians knew what the real issue involved—Cold War dominance.

In the late 1950s and early 1960s, the United States, with its vast economic resources, created a mammoth crash program to achieve superiority in outer space. Two motives reinforced each other: the need to stay ahead of the Soviets on the military security front and the immense possibilities space created for peaceful and commercial uses. These two imperatives have been in competition throughout the ensuing fifty years of space exploration.

In the 1960s, the attention of the world focused on achievements related to the scientific exploration of the universe. For a while, the Soviets maintained their position as frontrunners, launching the first human, Yuri Gagarin, into space in 1961. A year later, the United States responded by launching the first American astronaut, John Glenn. In the years that followed, the achievement of one country was quickly matched by the other. Finally, on July 20, 1969, after an enormously expensive program, U.S. superiority was symbolized when astronauts Neil A. Armstrong and Edwin E. Aldren Jr. landed on the Moon.

In the scientific exploration of space, and later in its commercial uses, people understood space as a venue for developing a new world order based on international cooperation, rather than as a battlefield. In the United States, the vehicle for this progress was the

National Aeronautics and Space Administration (NASA), created by President Eisenhower in 1958. Although technically assigned the dual role of advancing national security and establishing cooperation in outer space exploration, within months the new agency was focused almost exclusively on scientific cooperation, leaving the military uses of outer space to the Department of Defense and its contractors. NASA helped the United States to develop space probes and began to use outer space as the observation station for understanding the solar system, our galaxy, and the universe.[2]

For the most part, NASA worked cooperatively with other countries through an international organization, the Committee on Space Research (COSPAR) of the International Council of Scientific Unions. COSPAR was established in 1958 to provide an apolitical venue for international cooperation in outer space. Its task was to set standards for scientific research, to present findings to the world scientific community, and to advise international organizations as they attempted to set rules and guidelines for the exploration and use of outer space. COSPAR's main aim was to foster scientific cooperation among scientists outside of the tense military rivalries of their governments. From the very beginning of the space age, the United States, often working through COSPAR, cooperated with other nations by sharing scientific information, training personnel, launching foreign satellites with U.S. rockets, and including other nations' experiments on U.S. satellites.

International cooperation in outer space exploration was advanced by both President John F. Kennedy and Soviet Chairman Nikita Khrushchev.[3] On the occasion of the first orbital flight by an American, John Glenn, Khrushchev wrote in his congratulatory telegram to Kennedy on February 21, 1962: "If our countries pooled their efforts—scientific, technical, and material—to explore outer space, this would be beneficial to the advancement of science and would be acclaimed by all peoples who would like to see scientific achievements benefit man and not be used for 'cold war' purposes and the arms race."

Kennedy wrote back the next day, "I am instructing the appropriate officers of this Government to prepare new and concrete proposals for immediate projects of common action, and I hope that at a very early date our representatives may meet to discuss our ideas and yours in a spirit of practical cooperation."[4] Somewhat successful negotiations then yielded the Bilateral Space Agreement of 1962, which called for "coordinated" rather than fully cooperative projects in the fields of weather, magnetic field mapping of the sun, and communication satellites. In light of the Cold War, no classified data would be exchanged, and no funds or equipment would be provided by either side to the other; however, scientific projects could be devised so that national programs of the two countries could independently explore common topics.

The idea of full cooperation was still enticing, and on September 20, 1963, President Kennedy proposed, in a speech at the United Nations, that the United States cooperate with the Soviets on a manned lunar flight. But this proposal was never implemented, due undoubtedly to the fact that such cooperation would compromise classified technology on both sides.

Though carefully guarding classified material, and hedging on full cooperation, the United States and the Soviet Union, now the Russian Federation, have jointly launched satellites and exchanged scientific information for almost half a century, and have recently worked together on the International Space Station. Both counties have recognized that outer space research is so complex that no one country can undertake it alone. The perspective that space exploration affords on life on earth has no doubt fostered cooperation also. As scientific research advanced, human beings saw themselves as residing together, regardless of nationality, on a planet that was itself a small bit of dust in an increasingly large universe, now measured in billions of light years. Today, as the United States moves toward space weaponization, and toward a stance of military unilateralism, it is important to understand how very different that stance is from what was originally a collaborative approach.

At the same time that the United States, the Soviet Union, and a growing number of other states were exploring outer space for scientific purposes, these countries were developing a wide range of revolutionary commercial services reliant on the use of outer space, including a worldwide communication system, a worldwide location system, and a global system of weather mapping and prediction. These services have involved the sharing of technology and operating systems with all the countries on the earth, the establishment of multinational corporations, and joint satellite ventures by over fifty cooperating countries. Today, these endeavors are providing hundreds of billions of dollars in worldwide revenue, and the infrastructure for commercial services that are transforming the global economy.

The militarization and weaponization of space are fundamentally at odds with constructive commercial and scientific projects. War in space would destroy the intrinsic trust and cooperation necessary to maintain these systems, and combat itself in space would produce debris that would destroy the satellites, seriously eroding the possibility of using space for peaceful purposes. Beyond this, because many communication and location functions of satellites serve both commercial and military purposes, satellites become targets, either in a space war or in an effort by one nation attempting to achieve military dominance in outer space.

Despite continuing collaboration in outer space exploration, the primary motivation of both the United States and the Soviet Union for entering outer space was neither scientific nor commercial, but military. Even prior to satellites, history had already suggested a powerful military use of outer space. At the end of World War II, the Germans used V-2 rockets to rain terror on England. These missiles left their launching pads in Germany, and then, following a highly arched path, landed on their hapless English targets. During such an attack, whole buildings or parts of city blocks would suddenly explode, struck by an enemy at launch stations hundreds of miles away.

While these terror weapons were highly inaccurate and at the time of little military value, they sketched out a disturbing picture of what warfare might look like in the future. Tanks could be halted, planes could be shot down in flight, but once launched, V-2 rockets could not be stopped. With better guidance and more powerful payloads, such rockets could become the "ultimate weapon."

This lesson was not lost on military planners in the Soviet Union or the United States. In 1952, under the guidance of Dr. Edward Teller, a Hungarian refugee who had come to the United States in 1935, the United States developed the H-bomb. And in 1957, the Soviets perfected the first intercontinental ballistic missiles (ICBMs), enabling them to hit targets in the United States from bases within the Soviet Union. In response to the "missile gap," the United States developed its own ICBMs in 1959, beginning with the Atlas D. The effort was advanced by Wernher von Braun, who had helped the Nazis develop the V-2 rocket. By 1962, the United States pulled ahead of the Soviet Union in the race to achieve superiority in ICBMs, and America has held its missile advantage ever since.[5] At the same time, the United States and the Soviet Union started to experiment with ground-based and space-based weapons designed to destroy the ICBMs. Missile defense would become a major preoccupation for both countries until they realized that they could not develop an effective system, and that missile defense itself, by creating uncertainty about how many ICBMs would get through, upped the costs of maintaining a system of mutual deterrence.

Beyond bombs and missiles, satellite development, following the downing of an American U-2 spy plane in 1960, has been a focus of both the American and Soviet space race programs, with satellites serving as spies, targeters, and monitors of arms control agreements. And once spy satellites were placed in orbit, both the United States and the Soviet Union began to experiment with anti-satellite weapons. In 1963, the United States established two anti-satellite (ASAT) systems in the Pacific Ocean and maintained them for almost ten years. The Soviets tested their own anti-satellite system using anti-satellites in orbit. The United States also developed an ASAT that could be launched from an F-15 aircraft to hit satellites in low-earth orbit.[6]

From 1958 to 1962, the United States also tested its ability to knock out spy satellites using nuclear explosions in space. The tests caused considerable damage to the earth's electromagnetic field and blacked out radio and television communication on the West Coast and in the Pacific region for several hours following each test. Finally, in 1962 the United States exploded the Starfish, a 1.4 megaton nuclear bomb—over one hundred times the force of the bomb dropped on Hiroshima—in space. This test was so powerful that it knocked out the power grid in Hawaii and disabled three satellites in low-earth orbit.[7]

While this and earlier tests had shown the capacity of a nuclear blast to knock out satellites, the side effects of space-based nuclear explosions were unacceptable. Such tests were banned in 1963, when President Kennedy, deeply concerned about the medical consequences of radioactive fallout from the above-ground nuclear weapons tests, initiated the Limited Test Ban Treaty, forbidding the testing of nuclear weapons on the earth, on the sea, in the atmosphere, and in outer space. This treaty, proposed and universally adopted in the United Nations, had one major flaw—it permitted underground nuclear explosions. Via this loophole, development and testing of nuclear weapons continued unabated. The Limited Test Ban is still in operation, although for some years most of the rest of the world has supported a Comprehensive Test Ban Treaty, which would include the prohibition of underground explosions. The United States, China, Iran, and Israel have signed but not ratified the Comprehensive Test Ban Treaty; India and Pakistan have neither signed nor ratified it, and North Korea has withdrawn from it.

The desire to militarize space, and eventually launch satellite weapons in space has historically been limited by the concept of mutual deterrence, unofficially called Mutual Assured Destruction, or MAD. MAD had effectively prevented war, because the offensive capability of blowing up the earth with hydrogen bombs had far outpaced the defensive capability—the ability of the United States and the Soviets to prevent these weapons from reaching their targets. ICBMs that could deliver hydrogen bombs constituted the "ultimate weapon," not only because of their destructive power—a hydrogen bomb could flatten a whole city, killing millions in a single blast and rendering the territory a radioactive wasteland—but also because they were unstoppable.

While World Wars I and II were incredibly destructive—the full casualty list for World War II has been calculated as high as 100 million—these deaths were incremental, created over months and years, not minutes. Armies fought it out on battlefields, gaining and losing territory; even the saturation bombing of cities that killed hundreds of thousands of innocent civilians was slower by orders of magnitude in producing deaths than the unimaginable horror of a nuclear attack. By contrast, the entire Cold War was conducted with the notion that a full military confrontation was simply not a viable option. Such a move on either side would result in the destruction of both antagonists. The nightmare estimates from the Rand Corporation of 100 to 200 million dead would actually happen. Despite numerous negotiations and conferences, the capacity to inflict unacceptable casualties on the other side still obtains today, as both the United States and Russia still maintain thousands of missiles on full alert, even with the Cold War having passed into history.

During the Cold War, outer space satellites offered the means to maintain a tenuous peace. They provided the information necessary to monitor the launching of missiles, and were designed to give the other side ample warning that missiles were coming. Satellites also provided the basis for direct contact between Washington and Moscow through the "hot line," which was installed on satellites in September 1971. With such communication, any misunderstandings relating to false missile launches could be handled immediately, and war thus averted. Satellites could also monitor the missile launch sites to detect whether an actual launch had taken place.[8]

Experiments in outer space weaponization—although limited and never reaching the stage of full deployment—continued to be conducted by both superpowers over the next three decades following Sputnik, until the breakup of the Soviet Union in 1989. For example, satellites might be used to destroy the launching stations of missiles, using nuclear explosives or directed (laser) energy. Orbiting satellites (tested in the early 1960s) could be used to shoot down or dismantle the satellites of other countries, or could discharge bombs or rockets onto targets on the earth. Permanent military stations could be sited on the Moon, or other celestial bodies.

These provocative notions caused great concern and ushered in a new era of international agreements designed to regulate and constrain the military uses of outer space. In the area of disarmament, the United Nations emerged in the 1950s as the global organization responsible for negotiating these treaties. Established in 1945, at the end of World War II, the UN was designed to take up the mantle of the failed League of Nations, and to "save succeeding generations from the scourge of war." Starting with the first significant nuclear disarmament negotiations following Hiroshima and Nagasaki, the UN went on to negotiate arms control treaties over the next five decades. As the world sought an international regime for outer space, the UN would become the primary focus for this effort as well.

In addition to the United Nations itself, a number of its specialized agencies would provide the venues for important international agreements and cooperation. The most important of these was the International Telecommunications Union (ITU), one of whose tasks was to handle the complex work of coordinating international telecommunications in outer space. Today, the ITU is responsible for the allocation of radio frequencies to be used between ground stations and satellites, and the assigning of orbital slots for satellites. The International Court of Justice (ICJ), established by the UN Charter in 1945 as a UN specialized agency, provided the first post–World War II international court for disputes over questions involving outer space. Over the decades, the ICJ has done valuable work, both in interpreting UN procedures and in settling disputes between nations, despite the fact that nations must agree to its jurisdiction in particular cases. Other UN specialized agencies, such as the International Civil Aviation Organization, the Universal Postal Union, the Maritime Union, and the World Health Organization, have focused on the uses of outer space communications in their respective fields. As the Bush administration undermines the UN's operations and authority in ways large and small, it is important to remember that in the field of outer space, the UN continues to be the world's principal international forum.

When the space age began in the late 1950s, nations looked increasingly to the United Nations for a new set of laws to control outer space and prevent a possible arms race. The models statesmen considered included the Chicago Convention on International Civil Aviation of 1944 and ongoing conventions regulating shipping on the high seas. Curiously, the model that came to be used was neither of these, but the Antarctic Treaty of 1959, an international treaty signed initially between nations that had cooperated closely in scientific exchanges during the International Geophysical Year (IGY), just the year before. Over sixty countries cooperated during the IGY, investigating the physics of the upper atmosphere, the earth's heat and water regimen, and the earth's structure and shape. The

IGY was probably the most intensive program of international scientific cooperation the world had ever seen and was viewed as the model for future multilateral cooperation in other areas, including outer space.[9]

The IGY's Antarctic Treaty of 1959 prohibited military operations, nuclear explosions, and the disposal of radioactive waste in Antarctica, and provided for cooperation in scientific operations and exchange of data. It also suspended claims of national ownership to sections of Antarctica, although it did not abolish these claims, and it allowed for mutual inspection of facilities.

Translocating the freezing wastes of Antarctica into outer space, in 1959, the United Nations established the UN Committee on the Peaceful Uses of Outer Space (COPUOS). This committee began the complex work of starting to define space law in the face of intense rivalry between the United States and the Soviet Union by dividing the committee's membership with exquisite care between pro-U.S., pro-Soviet, and neutral UN delegations. From then on, COPUOS, with strong U.S. leadership, became one of the principal venues for political and legal negotiations in outer space. Thus, simultaneous to militarizing outer space and building up its own nuclear arsenal, the United States took the lead in establishing laws for outer space and treaties for nuclear disarmament.

In 1963, using language mostly developed in COPUOS, the UN General Assembly unanimously passed a "Declaration of Legal Principles Governing the Activities of States in the Exploration and Use of Outer Space." It declared that:

- The exploration and use of outer space shall be carried on for the benefit and in the interests of all people;
- Outer space is free for exploration and use by all States on the basis of equality and in accordance with international law;

- No sovereignty or ownership can be claimed in space;
- Objects and persons launched into space should be returned promptly and safely if they land in a foreign country;
- Nations launching objects are responsible for damages caused by them; and
- Astronauts are "envoys of mankind," and that States should render to them all possible assistance if they are in trouble, and return them if they land in their territory.

These provisions followed very closely the model of the Antarctic Treaty. The passage of this important resolution came less than two months after another General Assembly resolution called on states to refrain from placing nuclear and other weapons of mass destruction in orbit or installing them on celestial bodies, such as the Moon or Mars. Although these were only resolutions, and not enforceable, they clearly expressed the will of the world community, and looked toward treaties that would directly obligate signatory nations. The Limited Test Ban was also passed in 1963, prohibiting nuclear testing in the atmosphere, underwater, and in outer space, the first treaty to make explicit reference to outer space.[10]

Despite the success of the UN General Assembly resolutions, the world still lacked a law for outer space, beyond the single provision of the Limited Test Ban Treaty. Such a law materialized four years later in 1967, with the passage of the "Treaty on Principles Governing the Activities of States in the Exploration and Use of Outer Space, including the Moon and other Celestial Bodies," commonly known as the Outer Space Treaty. This treaty, which followed the general principles of the 1963 General Assembly Resolution, functions as the "Magna Carta" of outer space.

The Outer Space Treaty is still in operation today and, while flawed in several respects, is the single most comprehensive attempt to codify the appropriate uses of outer space and forbid illegitimate ones. The language of the treaty, set out at the dawn of the space age, unequivocally endorses cooperation, peace, and hope with respect to outer space. While it does not prohibit the orbiting of weapons that are *not* weapons of mass destruction, and has no verification procedures, it does lay down a body of international law covering a number of important issues and provides direction for avoiding an outer space arms race.

The treaty's preamble, while not binding, sets a tone for what follows: it speaks of "great prospects opening up before mankind as a result of man's entry into outer space," of "the common interest of all mankind" in space exploration, and the use of space for "peaceful purposes." The treaty then lays out a set of binding articles:

The first article of the Outer Space Treaty is a declaration shunning selfish nationalism in the exploration and use of outer space, declaring that exploration "shall be carried out for the benefit and in the interests of all countries, irrespective of their degree of economic or scientific development, and shall be the province of all mankind." Outer space research, like cancer research or quantum mechanics, was to be a scientific pursuit for the participation of all nations with the outcomes and benefits accruing to all mankind.

The second article settles the issue of who owns outer space: "Outer space, including the Moon and other celestial bodies, is not subject to national appropriation by claim of sovereignty, by means of use or occupation, or by any other means." Unlike the new world of 1492, the modern counterparts of King Ferdinand and Queen Isabella will not own outer space. Where the sixteenth and seventeenth centuries saw European powers arming themselves to seize the lands of the New World, no such process, the treaty declared, will take place in outer space. Outer space will be the province for all humankind, not the separate domain of individual countries. This treaty definitively declares that we are all heirs to this vast realm of space, and that it exists for the benefit of all of us.

The treaty also declares that outer space will not become a

venue for nuclear war or a venue for other weapons of mass destruction. The fourth article declares that parties will not "place in orbit around the earth any objects carrying nuclear weapons or any other kinds of weapons of mass destruction, install such weapons on celestial bodies, or station such weapons in outer space in any other manner." While prohibiting nuclear weapons and weapons of mass destruction, the treaty does not prohibit conventional weapons in space, and this is the legal basis upon which the United States, still party to the 1967 Outer Space Treaty, is now developing orbital weapons. This stunning omission occurred because the U.S. Department of Defense refused to accept a total ban on weapons in space, and the State Department was forced to accede to Defense's demands.[11]

The use of outer space to orbit satellites that will bombard the earth with nuclear weapons is in clear violation of the treaty, as is use of the Moon or any other body to station such weapons, although the treaty does not forbid the use of military personnel for scientific research.

The treaty also settles the important questions of what should be done with astronauts and space vehicles that land on the territory of other states. It says that parties "shall regard astronauts as envoys of mankind in outer space and shall render to them all possible assistance in the event of accident, distress, or emergency landing on the territory of another State Party or on the high seas."

In its ninth article, the treaty calls for international consultation if the activity of one nation in outer space is likely to cause harm to the outer space facilities of another nation. This is fast becoming an important provision, as the United States and other nations develop anti-satellites (ASATS) to disrupt or shoot down the satellites of other countries. Such activities, designed to cause harm to the satellites of other countries, require prior international consultation under the treaty. This provision also applies to pieces of satellites or launch vehicles—debris—that may harm other satellites or, if they fall to earth, create damage there. Such debris is created by the testing or deployment of missile defense systems and anti-satellite defense weapons.

Finally, the treaty calls for full reporting on outer space activities, and the rights of mutual inspection of facilities. It declares that outer space is to be an open book, not the venue for secrecy and deception. There can be no secret bases in outer space or on the Moon. (For the full text of the 1967 Treaty, see Appendix 2.)

Despite its limitations, the Outer Space Treaty represents a remarkable achievement. At the time it was signed, nations had every expectation that its limitations would be quickly corrected, and that a peaceful regime would be established for outer space. Today, the United Nations is attempting to address the omissions in the treaty with a still more comprehensive treaty prohibiting all orbital weapons and providing verification procedures.[12] Yet for eight years, a U.S. veto has prevented the Geneva-based Conference on Disarmament from engaging in negotiating an international treaty prohibiting weapons in space.

Meanwhile, other treaties signed in the interim since the Outer Space Treaty went into effect in the late 1960s have supplemented and bolstered this initial effort. For example, the United Nations, in December of 1979, generated the "Agreement Governing the Activities of States on the Moon and other Celestial Bodies," known as the "Moon Treaty." The purpose of the Moon Treaty was defined in its preamble "to prevent the moon from becoming an area of international conflict," though its provisions would apply not only to the Moon but to all other celestial bodies.

This treaty stipulates that all celestial bodies are off limits to any military activity—for bases, weapons testing, or the orbiting of weapons of mass destruction. The Moon Treaty also rules out any national claims for the Moon and other celestial bodies. In its eleventh article, it states, "Neither the surface nor the subsurface of the Moon, nor any part thereof or natural resources in place, shall become property of any State, international intergovernmental or non-governmental organization, national organization or non-governmental entity or of any natural person." It also requires that exploitation of the Moon's natural resources be governed by an international regime and that resources be shared by all parties to the treaty. To ensure that the provisions of the treaty are honored, the treaty provides for the right of mutual inspection of all facilities or stations on the Moon.

While the Moon Treaty is a logical extension of the 1967 Outer Space Treaty, and repeats a number of its provisions, the United States, Russia, China, Great Britain, and most of the countries of the world have not ratified it. As the United States moves toward new landings on the Moon, and, as President Bush announced on January 14, 2004, possibly on Mars, the lure of economic exploitation, left open by the failure of nations to sign the Moon Treaty, threatens to come to the fore, just as commercial interests, including gold and spices, motivated the voyages of Columbus and Magellan, and the colonization of the New World that followed.

The United States has, however, ratified a number of other agreements, including treaties concerning "the Rescue of Astronauts, the Return of Astronauts and the Return of Objects Launched into Outer Space," "International Liability for Damage Caused by Space Objects," and "Registration of Objects Launched into Outer Space." While the Rescue of Astronauts and Liability agreements appear to be working well, the Registration agreement is incomplete, as it has no time limit on when satellites are to be registered, and for the most part states have not indicated if the purpose of their launches is military.[13]

While international law has attempted to restrict the use of outer space for military purposes, outer space has also continued to play an important role in arms control agreements. In the last decades of the Cold War, while the United States and the Soviet Union cut back their armaments through bilateral agreement, and forbade the use of intermediate range missiles, satellite observation was crucial in maintaining compliance.

Outer space continues to be a vital mechanism for monitoring arms control agreements in the future. Before satellites were deployed, arms control and disarmament agreements were often limited by the means of verification. How could the United States or the Soviets detect cheating by the other side if they could not actually see and monitor each other's territory? The problem was solved when satellites could overfly the nations in space without violating their national airspace, so that once unenforceable treaties could now be put into practice. For example, a bilateral agreement between the United States and the Soviet Union, the 1971 "Agreement on Measures to Reduce the Risk of Outbreak of Nuclear War," required both sides "to notify each other immediately in the event of detection by missile warning systems of unidentified objects, or in the event of signs of interference with these systems or with related communications facilities, if such occurrences could create a risk of outbreak of nuclear war between the two countries." The agreement also required the parties to provide each other advance notification "of any planned missile launches if such launches will extend beyond its national territory in the direction of the other party." A number of treaties still use this technique, which is made increasingly effective by instant observations and communication through satellites, for reducing the risk of nuclear war.[14]

Yet despite the growth of international law and treaties looking to the peaceful uses of outer space, the United States, in particular, the most technologically sophisticated country in the world, continued to explore expanding military uses of outer space throughout the last decades of the twentieth century. Decades of military research finally surfaced in the 1990s, when outer space satellites became involved not only in target identification but in a whole new area: guiding weapons to their targets.

This capacity was first demonstrated during the Persian Gulf War of 1991. The accuracy of satellite-guided bombs and missiles was radically different from aerial bombing in World War II, where the allies had relied on a massive number of bombs to destroy particular targets. Even during the Korean War, bombs could only be expected to hit within 300 meters of their intended target. Satellite-guided bombs and missiles, by contrast, used space-determined coordinates to achieve a degree of precision hitherto unknown.

By the time of the 1991 Gulf War, "smart bombs" using satellite-guided lasers accounted for only 4.3 percent of the total tonnage dropped, but inflicted 75 percent of the damage.[15] Such weapons were orders of magnitude more accurate than those of World War II, Korea, or Vietnam. Richard L. Garwin, Senior Fellow for Science and Technology at the Council on Foreign Relations, and a member of the 1998 Rumsfeld Commission, describes the global positioning system for navigating vehicles and for guiding homing bombs and missiles as so precise that the guided weapon "could strike in the middle of the room and not the edge of the room, and if you wanted, it could strike to centimeter accuracy."[16]

Such weapons reduce the need to jeopardize the lives of soldiers on the ground or pilots in the air, though they can incur terrible destruction upon their targets. Kosovo, in 1999, was the first war in history where the overwhelming mass of casualties involved little or no risk on the inflicting side. This was repeated in the 2003 Iraq War in which the United States used smart bombs almost exclusively. These weapons can be used in bad weather, can be fired from extreme distances, no longer require pilots to guide them, and are relatively inexpensive—a bonanza of long-distance killing, courtesy of space-based satellites. In summary, space-guided munitions can radically minimize casualties among the attacking forces but they can claim disproportionate deaths and casualties among innocent civilians who may happen to be captured by waves of these indiscriminate weapons that rain down on them.

If a target can be detected by satellite or plane, it can be destroyed, including armored bunkers and fortified positions. Wars fought by technically superior countries, such as the United States, now entail virtually no risk to their own personnel, although as aforementioned, this immunity does not apply to inhabitants of the conquered territory. The capacity to wage war without risk of major casualties to its armed forces, made possible by satellite guidance, has totally changed the calculus of foreign relations.[17] (It is, however, important to note that U.S. soldiers are suffering a relatively high death and casualty rate as they are specifically targeted by various sectors of the Iraqi society. This degree of destruction is small in magnitude compared with the enormous number of Iraqi civilian casualties.)

As the United States has perfected its technical capacities in weapons guidance, it has once again undertaken the development of missile defense, after sidelining missile defense during the 1990s. Shorter-range missile defenses called theater defenses, which do not enter outer space, are designed to be used in battlefield conditions or to intercept missiles launched from ships and submarines. In addition, the United States is again spending billions of dollars installing a long-range system of missile defense to stop Intercontinental Ballistic Missiles aimed at the United States (see Chapter 3). This is a system that tracks its targets—other countries' missiles traversing outer space, and "kills" or destroys with a kinetic impact.[18] The technology developed for ICBMs and missile defense has become the basis for future extensions of combative power in outer space—satellites designed to shoot down the satellites of other countries, and satellites designed to bombard the earth.

As we embark on the twenty-first century, the United States is also developing weapons to be directly deployed in outer space, and has resisted all international efforts to ban such weapons by treaty. As the United States moves toward space weaponization, other nations, particularly Russia and China, are beginning to develop the means to counter these weapons, or put up weapons of their own—(see Chapter 4). So ironically, the very concept of weapons in space, even before they are deployed, has already led to the beginnings of a frightening global escalation of force.

If the United States does indeed weaponize the heavens, it will put at risk the entire new world of global communications, weather prediction, mapping and location, and scientific exploration. And weapons once employed will eventually be used; that is the history of the human race. If that history is not to repeat itself, we must act now to preserve the precious assets we have developed in outer space, let alone life on earth.

2

The Peaceful Potential of Outer Space

When I consider your heavens,
the work of your fingers,
the moon and the stars,
which you have set in place,
what is man that you are mindful of him,
the son of man that you care for him?

—Psalm 8:3–4

With regard to space dominance, we have it, and we
like it, and we're going to keep it.

—Keith Hall, the U.S. Air Force Assistant Secretary
for Space and Director of the National
Reconnaissance Office[1]

The Report of the Weapons of Mass Destruction Commission, chaired by Dr. Hans Blix, states, "The world now relies on space technology for security and other purposes such as meteorology, environmental monitoring, disaster prevention, communications, education, entertainment and surveillance."[2] Outer space has created a set of services so sweeping, so part of our lives, that most people simply accept them as they accept gravity or sunlight. One of the key components of modern globalization is precisely these services. Without them, today's world would revert back to a collection of national sovereign states loosely connected by international alliances, trade agreements, and inefficient means of communication.

Fifty years ago, we thought of the world as composed of isolated countries and areas, with their own completely different languages, cultures, economies, separated by impassible barriers of space, and inaccessible to affordable communication. Today, we think of the world as one planet. In the United States, we think nothing of talking on a regular basis to someone in Australia fourteen time zones away.

Each person is a neighbor. We cannot anymore pretend that the fate of people in other countries can be outside our moral consciousness. If someone is starving in Nigeria, or suffering from AIDS, he or she is our moral neighbor, and his or her fate is part of our collective responsibility. For the history of humankind, this responsibility was limited by knowledge, distance, and communication. Today, those limits have disappeared, and we are part of one human family. If this responsibility has not been recognized by our governments, it is our duty to insist that, with the knowledge, communication, and accessibility possible, we are indeed responsible and need to act.

We are also part of a single economy. Due to instant digital and voice communication, parts of products which once were produced entirely in only one country are now made in many, and assembled in still others; and international finances have united us with countries that once seemed remote and inaccessible. China and the United States, for example, share credit and product relationships in ways that were inconceivable at the dawn of the space age.

Equally, culture, which once was geographically defined, has now become international, with English the lingua franca of the world. While this has entailed the loss of much specifically local culture, young adults in Beijing, Lagos, Buenos Aires, or New York view the same DVDs, set up multilateral chat groups, and rock to the same music. America's greater technological reach and wealth have meant that American commercial culture tends to be dominant at the start of this century.

This homogenization of culture is in a sense tragic because the multiplicity of traditions, religious practices, music, folk lore, cuisines, and clothing was the very essence of the wonders of the broad human experience.

These developments in cultural and commercial outreach were foreseen at the very dawn of the space age, when businessmen in the United States saw the almost infinite possibilities offered by outer space communication. Today the commercial "space sector" provides the United States over $100 billion a year in direct revenue, and many times that in the myriad sectors of the economy that are supported by satellite service.[3] For every dollar spent on space research, $7 will be returned to the U.S. Treasury in the form of personal and corporate income taxes provided by jobs and economic growth.[4]

The principal agents of this revolution are communication satellites—COMSATs—which usually operate from geosynchronous orbits about 22,300 miles above the earth. These satellites orbit in outer space at approximately the same speed as the earth turns so they are virtually stationary. Broadcasts from a satellite in geosynchronous orbit can cover only about a third of the earth, so three satellites in geosynchronous orbit are usually needed to service the whole earth. Some recent systems also utilize a series of low-earth orbiting satellites. Earth-based satellite dishes, called earth stations or teleports, are used to transmit or receive messages. Space-based communication satellites are complementary to fiber optic submarine communication undersea cables, although their costs are considerably lower— $175 million for an undersea cable versus $80 million for a satellite.

The United States was the first country to launch a communication satellite when it chartered a public/private hybrid called the COMSAT Corporation and, in 1964, established the International Telecommunications Satellite Consortium (INTELSAT) with COMSAT having majority control.[5] INTELSAT continues to be the biggest worldwide satellite communication network, including 110 nations, and providing service to over 600 earth stations in more than 149 countries, territories, and dependencies. Domestic satellites are used to provide telecommunication services such as voice, data, and video transmission within a country.[6]

The International Telecommunications Union (ITU), a specialized agency of the UN, coordinates much of this system. In the 1990s, the ITU was expanded to include private companies, which became members with participation rights equal to nation-states. One of the services provided by the ITU is the allocation of radio frequencies used by the communication systems.

The first communication satellite was Project SCORE, launched in December of 1958 and used by President Eisenhower to send a proud Christmas greeting to the world. The first commercial communications satellites were launched in 1965. These were followed by a series of active satellites that receive signals from earth, electronically strengthen them, and then transmit the signals back to the ground. These satellites are used by cable and TV networks to distribute their programming to local affiliate stations within a specific country, as well as globally. They are also used for long-distance telephone, radio, e-mail, and Web sites. Satellite services provide the infrastructure for cell phones, wireless Internet service, and 24/7 satellite-distributed news and entertainment.

A worldwide system of communication has unified the planet in ways that were inconceivable half a century ago. Not only may individuals communicate with each other at extremely low cost, but planetary organizations are now possible through phone and Web communications, such as the network of international non-governmental organizations that provided the basis for the 1997 Kyoto Protocol on climate control through the regulation of carbon gas emissions. Today civil society is worldwide, not just national, and can deal with such planetary issues.

Satellites provide an alternative communication system that national governments cannot completely control. Satellite communications, for example, created the basis for the 1989 Tiananmen Square protests in China, and in countries like Russia provide an alternative civil society in the context of a government that dominates the press, radio, and television. Complete government control of communications, a la Nazi Germany or Stalinist Russia, is no longer possible.

On the commercial front, satellite communication instantly posts orders, receipts, and shipments, and can transmit digital plans for factories and machinery to the farthest corners of the globe. While this allows expertise to be shared internationally, this kind of communication can also be put to less noble purposes including allowing wealthy nations, such as the United States, to operate plants in countries where wages are considerably lower, often with attendant social costs.

Satellite communication has also created a global news system, which operates at twice the speed of the pre-space era. News that once seemed remote becomes part of our daily lives, including reports of the breakdown of government in East Timor or revolts in Somalia. The insularity of national culture is a relic of another era.

Finally, satellite communication brings entertainment to other countries at virtually no cost. In the poorest parts of Central America or Africa, families without shoes or chairs sit in the dirt watching American television or dance to American music. At the same time, by creating a worldwide consumer market for American culture, the United States effaces local cultures and customs as discussed above.

A major function of satellites is to provide exact location coordinates. Before satellites became available, only the most primitive mechanisms existed to determine the precise location of airplanes, ships, automobile drivers, and the like. Collisions of planes or ships are virtually impossible today. With the assistance of satellites, pilots, ship captains, and ordinary individuals can track their courses and pinpoint their positions with absolute accuracy. Since radio was invented at the end of the nineteenth century, ships at sea have relied on Morse code for distress and safety telecommunications. After the

Titanic sank in the North Atlantic in 1912, the U.S. Congress enacted legislation requiring U.S. ships to use Morse code radiotelegraph equipment for distress calls. The International Telecommunications Union, established in 1934, also required such communications for ships of all nations. Morse encoded distress calling has saved thousands of lives since it was first used almost a century ago, but it required skilled radio operators spending many hours listening to the radio distress frequency, and the system itself could carry only a limited number of messages.

To get a better system, in 1979, a group of experts drafted the International Convention on Maritime Search and Rescue, which called for the development of a global search and rescue plan utilizing the new asset of outer space satellites. The new system, the Global Maritime Distress Safety System, established by Canada, France, Russia, and the United States, increased safety and facilitated the rescue of distressed ships and aircraft. One satellite system is designed specifically to transmit to a rescue coordination center an accurate location of a distressed ship or airplane from anywhere in the world. Another provides emergency weather information. Satellites have thus led to a significant decrease in the hazards of international travel. A similar program, called Cospas-Sarsat, also started by the United States, Russia, Canada, and France, rescues individuals who may be lost or injured in the wilderness. The first rescue was in 1982, when somewhere in the rugged Rocky Mountains of British Columbia a small airplane was reported overdue. Rescue missions couldn't find the plane, but it was picked up by a Soviet COSMOS satellite, which then relayed the signal to a ground station in Ottawa. A team was dispatched from Ottawa and saved three lives. Since then improvements in the system have made its "ears in space" even more sensitive.[7] By September 9, 2005, the system had rescued 18,500 people.[8]

One of the most important organizations providing positioning and location services is the Global Positioning System (GPS), a satellite system designed and controlled by the U.S. Department of Defense. The first GPS satellite was launched in 1978, and the system reached full operational capability in 1995. GPS currently employs twenty-eight satellites, each of which orbits the earth every twelve hours, and costs about $400 million a year to maintain. These satellites can determine the location and time reference for almost any point on the earth or conversely for a satellite in earth orbit. A GPS receiver, which connects with the system, takes in signals from four satellites in order to determine its own latitude, longitude, elevation, and precise time.

Civilian GPS receivers cost only about $100, and these devices are now widely available for cars, airplanes, and ships, and for mountain climbers and hikers. Indeed, GPS has created a revolution in travel. Motorists can switch on their GPS to find out where they are, as can ship captains and airline pilots.[9] The GPS system is also used for aerial refueling and rendezvous, geodesic surveys, as well as search and rescue operations.

While satellites are providing exact location information, they are also mapping the world in ways that were impossible in the pre-satellite era. Fifty years ago, large areas of the world were inadequately mapped as such maps required the actual presence of people to do the mapping. The most basic descriptions of the topography and geography of deserts and mountain regions, jungles, and extensive stretches of coastline were missing. Today, we have precision maps of our entire planet via photos taken by satellite.

GPS maintains a worldwide common grid, supporting an unlimited number of users and areas, and GPS receivers can now monitor global ocean current circulations, determine the dynamic relationships between the oceans and atmosphere, and improve global climate predictions.[10] Although it is controlled by the U.S. Department of Defense, a major part of the Global Positioning System is available to anyone free of charge, or at nominal cost. However, like COMSATS and weather satellites, the Global Positioning System has dual military and civilian uses. The ability to pinpoint any spot on the earth can be used to locate a hiker or a military tank, to navigate on a cross-country vacation, and to spot a missile station or locate targets for attack. GPS's military potential was first put to the test in Operations Desert Shield and Desert Storm in 1990–91, where GPS provided accurate targeting for smart bombs, cruise missiles, and other munitions. Allied troops also relied heavily on GPS to navigate the featureless desert. During this war, forward air controllers, pilots, and tank drivers used the system so successfully that several U.S. defense officials said that GPS was the key to the Desert Storm victory.[11]

A section of the GPS system is used exclusively by the U.S. military for itself or its allies, and in a war zone the Pentagon can jam civilian GPS units while allowing the military full use. The U.S. military reserves the right to limit the signal strength or the accuracy of the GPS system, or to shut down GPS completely, so it cannot be available to unwanted users during a time of conflict. However, GPS is highly vulnerable to jamming by other organizations or nations. It can also be "spoofed" by broadcast signals that deliberately provide misleading information, and it is vulnerable to unintentional interference from natural causes, such as solar flares and ionospheric scintillation, as well as TV broadcasts, military jamming/spoofing tests, and military communications systems. At present, however, the GPS is fairly immune to destruction by anti-satellite weapons, because it can lose up to four satellites without serious impairment.[12]

In December 2004, the United States released a directive on security concerns related to GPS uses. The directive called for the development of capabilities to "deny to adversaries position, navigation, and timing services from the Global Positioning System, its augmentations, and/or any other space-based position, navigation, and timing systems, without unduly disrupting civil, commercial, and scientific uses of these services outside an area of military operations, or for homeland security purposes."[13] The Europeans are so concerned about U.S. military control of the GPS that they are developing their own system, called Galileo, which is not yet operational.[14] In an early paper, dated December 31, 2001, the European Commission stated, "If the Galileo program is abandoned, we will, in the next 20 to 30 years, lose our autonomy in defense." A second paper, dated March 12, 2002, states, "If the EU finds it necessary to undertake a security mission that the U.S. does not consider to be in its interest, [the EU] will be impotent unless it has the satellite navigation technology that is now indispensable."

The decision to proceed with Galileo was made on May 26, 2003, by the European Union and the European Space Agency, at an estimated cost of $2.1 billion.[15] Thirty satellites will be launched from Galileo from 2006 to 2008, and the system will be operational in 2008, with two-thirds of the cost covered by private companies and investors, and the rest divided between the European Space Agency and the European Union. In addition to providing civilian services, Galileo will also offer an alternative service, allowing the EU a satellite-assisted military and police system of its own. Navigation signals from Galileo will work their way into the design of intelligence weapons, aircraft, ships, individual handheld units for soldiers, and unmanned surveillance systems.

Competition between Galileo and GPS could in the future provide troop movements and guerrilla actions with alternative satellite navigation systems. It could also result in destructive interference between the two systems. As reported by GPS World on September 24, 2005, "According to sources in the United States, all of whom asked not be named, the PRS [Galileo] signal as now envisioned could potentially interfere with GPS." An even more serious potential problem is mutual jamming of signals, although it is also possible that these problems can be worked out with through a diplomatic agreement.[16]

Tomas Valasek, director of the Brussels office of the U.S. Center for Defense Information, writes, "While the U.S. is working hard to ensure that future enemies will not have access to the GPS, the same does not hold true for Galileo. What if a hostile army used Galileo signals to guide missiles against Europeans forces? Or U.S. ones? The [European] Commission insists that 'there is no question here of coming into conflict with the United States.' But the prospect of the EU inadvertently aiding U.S. enemies is worrisome."[17]

Meanwhile, China and Israel have agreed to join the Galileo project, as have the Ukraine and India, although in January 2004, China was denied access to the Public Regulated Service government channel, which is Galileo's most secure channel, probably for security reasons.[18] At the same time, the Russians have developed their own system, called GLONASS. This system, like Galileo, gives the Russians military independence from the United States in this crucial area of outer space services. Because of the age-old problem of military competition, a number of essentially redundant world positioning systems are being developed, which, in turn, are creating their own tensions.

A parallel function of satellites to global positioning is monitoring and predicting the weather. In the past, weather monitoring was depressingly inaccurate because vast areas of the world, particularly the seas, the deserts, jungles, and the arctic regions, which influence global weather patterns, could not be monitored, just as many of these areas could not be mapped. Weather predictions were educated guesses at best, not scientific determinations, and they were frequently wrong. Today, for shipping, aviation, agriculture, sporting activities, and hikes in the woods, people can know with some dependable certainty what the weather will be and can plan accordingly.

Weather satellites primarily monitor weather and climate, but they also report fires, pollution, sand storms, ice flows, ocean currents, and energy waste, and relay other vital environmental information. For example, weather satellites monitored volcanic ash from Mount St. Helens, when the volcano erupted. Weather satellites have for the first time given our planet a system that is accurate and accessible to virtually every country and inhabitant.

Weather satellites can be geostationary or polar orbiting. The first successful weather satellite, TOROS-1, which orbited the earth, was launched by NASA in 1960. The United States, the Europeans, the Russians, and the Chinese all have weather satellites in geostationary orbit transmitting pictures. The United States, China, India, and Russia also have weather satellites that circle the earth over the poles, and can observe any place on earth and every location twice a day.

In addition to predicting the weather, these satellites map ocean currents valuable to the shipping industry, chart land, and provide water temperatures helpful to farmers interested in protecting their crops and to fishermen increasing their harvest from the sea. They also predict the amount of snow available for runoff vital to water sheds in places including the western United States. Some of the most dramatic satellite photos were of the oil-well fires started by Iraq as its troops fled Kuwait in February of 1991. A wide variety of weather satellite images are available to meteorologists or anyone with access to the Internet. While weather was once thought of as localized, and its prediction was inaccurate at best, we now have a system that works for every nation on earth. It is impossible to estimate the immense value of such information, although it could be placed in the tens of billions of dollars.

Satellite launching is a complex and expensive process unaffordable and beyond the technical reach of most countries of the world. A number of these countries use the governmental and private facilities of the space-launching countries to put their own satellites into outer space. Today, fifty-five countries have taken advantage of such arrangements, and although they lack space-launching capacity, they are able to participate directly in the use of outer space for their own commercial and scientific purposes. The current strength of European and Russian currencies means that these countries are now reaping most of the space-launching business, a factor that may be driving U.S. corporations into more military uses of space.[19]

Satellites are also launched for scientific purposes, and particularly in the twentieth century, science became a global enterprise, not confined to one country or even to one region of the world. In outer space, as perhaps in no other area, science exploration was conceived from the beginning as a global enterprise, and through COSPAR of the International Council of Scientific Unions, scientific findings are made available to any country desiring them.

Nowadays, sensitive equipment mounted on satellites is able to observe the farthest reaches of the universe; scientists can work for months at a time in orbital stations; and probes can reach distant planets and meteors. For the first time, we have the direct means to determine if there are signs of life on other planets, to analyze the chemical composition of meteors, to probe the formation and effect of "black holes," and to test theories on the origins of the universe.

Beyond satellite observation, science has moved to direct exploration of the solar system. Starting in 1962, the United States, followed closely by the Soviet Union, began exploring the nature of other planets, particularly Venus, Mars, and Mercury, culminating in soft landings on Mars in 1976. The primary focus was to determine if conditions to support life existed on Mars. Space probes explored the nature of the sun, and began to rendezvous with comets, the first being the Halley's comet in 1986, and to explore the outer planets, sending back spectacular pictures of Jupiter, Saturn, Uranus, and Neptune (1977). Space observation was given a huge boost in 1990, at a cost of $1.5 billion, when the United States launched the gigantic Hubble Space Telescope.

By the early 1970s, the United States had launched a space station, Skylab, in orbit for eight months, which facilitated long-term scientific research from outer space, including both astrophysical research and the study of the earth's natural resources. Solar flares were observed on the sun and its composition and chemistry determined with a new precision. On the earth, scientists were able to identify potentially productive land, map deserts, measure snow and ice cover, locate mineral deposits, trace marine and wildlife migration, and detect dangerous pollution. Skylab was followed by other U.S. and Russian space stations, culminating in the International Space Station, which is still under construction and is scheduled to be finished in 2010. This venture includes members of the European Space Agency and Russia, and is serviced by a U.S. and Russian crew. The Skylab is almost 300 feet long and weighs almost a million pounds. Although many countries are involved in the scientific exploration of outer space, the United States accounts today for about 70 percent of the action.

The future is exciting because the scientific exploration of outer space promises answers to major questions that have challenged mankind. What are the origins of the universe? What are the origins and nature of black holes? Are the laws of nature here on earth and in the solar system operational in other galaxies? Do life and intelligent beings exist in the hundred billion galaxies that scientists now see as our universe?

These questions will, in many ways, affect our entire thinking about the world. Just as the shift to Newtonian physics, or later to field physics and quantum mechanics, altered our perception of self and the psychology and history of ourselves in the world, so too will the findings of space exploration provide the substructure for sweeping new ventures in thought. If we find intelligent beings in other star systems, how will this affect our thoughts about human beings, previously the only creatures with advanced intelligence? If we have trouble relating to the Chinese or the Russians, how will we relate to inhabitants of another solar system? Can we extend the rule of law to other creatures? Can we craft a galactic diplomacy?[20]

Throughout the space age, prestige and international competition have warred with strictly scientific exploration. A recent example is President Bush's announcement, on January 14, 2004, of a plan for the United States to go to the Moon and Mars. Bush's

"Vision for Space Exploration" once again focuses on manned landings, after the U.S. success thirty-eight years ago in landing on the Moon. The cost of the total program has been set at $104 billion, with $12 billion being spent in the first five years.[21]

As the *Washington Post* reported, "The plan envisions development of two new rockets, one of them almost as tall and even heavier than the Saturn V that launched the Apollo astronauts, and a new spacecraft to put four people on the Moon for up to six months before bringing them back to Earth in a parachute landing. . . . The use of 'crew' and 'service' modules to orbit the Moon while astronauts travel to and from the surface in a 'lunar lander' called to mind the Apollo mission that put 12 men on the Moon between 1969 and 1972." The program will allow the astronauts to establish permanent bases on the Moon for the subsequent Mars mission. Competition is already keen between Northrop Grumman, Boeing, and Lockheed Martin for the right to build the exploration vehicle.[22]

In the plan, the Moon will be used as a launch pad for deeper space exploration, and might also provide resources to fuel or facilitate these missions. President Bush explained that the surface of the Moon "contains raw materials that might be harvested and processed into rocket fuel or breathable air." No date was indicated for the Mars mission, but the earliest estimated date would be 2030. As opposed to the earlier Apollo mission to the Moon, the president indicated that the United States would welcome international cooperation on the project. "We'll invite other nations to share the challenges and opportunities of this new era of discovery," he said. "The vision I've outlined today is a journey, not a race, and I call on other nations to join us on this journey, in the spirit of cooperation and friendship."[23]

The scientific community, however, does not unanimously endorse this blueprint for space exploration. The American Physical Society, the nation's primary organization of research physicists, for example, has responded by declaring that "very important scientific opportunities could be lost or delayed seriously as a consequence of shifting NASA priorities toward Moon-Mars." Most space scientists consider robotic missions to be equal, if not superior, to manned missions. While the American Physical Society did not directly attack the president for his declaration, its fuller statement makes clear its view of just how superficial and political the president's announcement was:

> We believe that human exploration also has a role to play in NASA, but it must be within a balanced program in which allocated resources span the full spectrum of space science and take advantage of emerging scientific opportunities and synergies. We further believe that our understanding of the moons and planets of our solar system takes its full significance only within the more global context of a systematic study of nature: from the early universe to the formation of planets around other stars; from the fundamental laws of physics to the emergence of life; from the relations between the sun and the planets to the complex interactions in ecological systems and the impact of humanity on its environment. Returning Americans to the Moon and landing on Mars would have a powerful symbolic significance, but it would constitute only a small step in the advancement of knowledge, since much will already be known from exploration with the robotic precursor probes that are necessary to guarantee the safety of any human mission.[24]

Meanwhile, the scientific basis of our space program is already being reduced. On March 2, 2006, the *New York Times* reported, "Some of the most highly promoted missions on NASA's scientific agenda would be postponed indefinitely or perhaps even canceled under the agency's new budget, despite its administrator's vow to Congress six months ago that not 'one thin dime' would be taken from space science to pay for President Bush's plan to send astronauts to the Moon and Mars."[25] And on April 10, 2005, the *Washington Post* reported that NASA is poised to pull funding from two space probes of the Voyager program which have been sending data back to earth since 1977 and are now at the outer reaches of the solar system. Its science reporter, Rick Weiss, sees this move as part of a general retreat from open-ended scientific research in a wide variety of fields in favor of

> specific products, profits or outcomes—"deliverables," in the parlance of the government. . . . But what about Voyager 1 and 2, which scientists say can probably keep operating until 2020? What good are they? Sure, their instruments have sent back 5 trillion bits of data and 80,000 pictures, including spectacular close-ups of Jupiter, Saturn, Uranus and Neptune and astonishing details from various moons—22 of which were previously undiscovered. Yes, they've been detecting the impacts of solar flares at the very edge of the sun's influence and are sensing for the first time what the rest of the universe is made of. But how in the world are we going to take that to the bank?

Weiss maintains that "our understanding of the world and our support of the quest for knowledge for knowledge's sake is a core measure of our success as a civilization."[26]

Although during the Cold War competition with the Soviets ranged over the entire area of armaments, public attention focused on the space race as a key index to determine which country was winning. With the Cold War over, the need for intense competition and spectacular results has ended. Today, with diminishing funds for research, and a possible shortfall in Americans trained in applicable sciences, it is increasingly important for the United States to forego unilateral prestige and take advantage of multilateral opportunities for cooperation with other countries in outer space research, prioritizing its expenditures for maximum scientific results.[27]

For any of the benefits of outer space mentioned in this chapter to be sustained and expanded, space must be secured for peaceful purposes. The weaponization of space would virtually destroy the peaceful uses of space, with enormous ramifications for global commerce, weather forecasting, and the like. The products of fifty years of industry and cooperation would be destroyed by war in space.

As the Bush administration continues its retreat to an outdated and inappropriate Cold War mentality, and moves toward the weaponization of space as a unilateral venture, the entire use of space for peaceful purposes is threatened. War in heaven can only impoverish life on earth.

Missile Defense: The Prelude to Space-Based Weapons

When I behold, upon the night's starr'd face,
Huge cloudy symbols of a high romance
—John Keats

Precision weapons guided to their targets by space-based navigation—instant global communications for commanders and their forces—enemy weapons of mass destruction held at risk by a ready force of intercontinental ballistic missiles—adversary ballistic missiles detected within seconds of launch. This is not a vision of the future. This is Space today!
—General Lance W. Lord, USAF Commander[1]

The first military use of outer space was the development of Intercontinental Ballistic Missiles (ICBMs). The second was defensive systems designed to stop them. Although the United States has invested approximately $150 billion in its development, missile defense against ICBMs has never worked.[2] Despite five decades of failure, the idea has continued to haunt military planners since the Cold War began.[3] While the dream—the idea that a bomb, once launched on a missile, could be stopped in mid-flight by another, very precisely aimed missile—never materialized, the history of missile defense offers a number of important insights into the extension of military power into outer space. Furthermore, much of the technology developed in ground-based missile defense is being exploited to design missile defense launched from outer space, and is also applicable to space weaponization.

Missile defense began at the end of World War II, when the Germans rained V-2 rockets on England. Although the V-2s did not win the war for Germany, after Hiroshima and Nagasaki military analysts understood that missiles, far more accurate and armed with nuclear warheads, would inevitably follow. The threat of such missiles prompted the United States to explore construction of a missile defense system.

As the United States and the Soviets developed their nuclear arsenals, they mounted their bombs onto missiles capable of traveling from one continent to another, and began to arm the missiles with ever-more-powerful weapons. Whereas the bombs dropped at Hiroshima and Nagasaki were in the kiloton range, or the equivalent of thousands of tons of TNT, hydrogen bombs brought nuclear explosions into an entirely different dimension, that of megatons, or the equivalent of *millions* of tons of TNT. As reported by International Physicians for the Prevention of Nuclear War, a single megaton weapon (one million tons of TNT equivalent) creates a crater 300 feet deep and 1,200 feet in diameter. Within one second, the atmosphere itself ignites into a fireball more than a half-mile in diameter. The surface of the fireball radiates nearly three times the light and heat of a comparable area of the surface of the sun, extinguishing all life below in seconds. When the United States developed hydrogen bombs in 1952, and the Soviets acquired them a year later, the world was forced to confront a possible doomsday scenario.

Secretary of Defense Robert McNamara first fully defined the concept of Mutual Assured Destruction (MAD) in a speech in 1962. If one side launched its nuclear armed missiles against the other, it was assumed that the damaged side would still have enough missiles left to inflict unacceptable levels of damage on the aggressor. From the start of the Cold War until the fall of the Soviet Union in

1989, MAD effectively prevented nuclear exchange between the two sides, although the blockade of Berlin in 1948–49 and the Cuban missile crisis in 1962 proved very close calls. While some people think that it was merely a matter of luck that the world survived nuclear destruction, this beneficial concept of MAD is the accepted wisdom even today.

Although MAD was deemed to be effective, both the United States and the Soviet Union began research on missile defense in the mid-1950s, and pursued it in earnest in the 1960s. But despite massive scientific research, neither side was able to develop an operational system.

One possible "defense" seemed obvious: to destroy the enemy's missile sites before they could launch a nuclear strike, a concept that required outer space satellites to identify the sites. But this posed a terrible danger. If a missile silo were destroyed in enemy territory, it had to be assumed that the enemy would then launch a nuclear attack with its remaining missiles.

Another "defense" would be the destruction of enemy missiles as they were leaving their launching pads. This seemed practical because the relative speed of the boost-phase missiles would be slow, and the missiles would not yet have had the opportunity to disguise their flight through deceptive decoys, which is possible in mid-course once the missile has left the atmosphere and entered outer space.

But the challenges of stopping a missile attack during the "boost-phase" are formidable. The decision to attack against enemy missiles in the boost-phase would have to be instantaneous and would leave almost no time to consider whether to move from peace to war. Such a decision would have to be made literally in seconds by a computer triggered by satellite detection with no human input. How could a decision that might end up vaporizing hundreds of millions of people be made in this way? What if the other side were actually launching peaceful scientific satellites that were misinterpreted as destructive missiles? The chance of a fatal mistake was too high. A boost-phase attack would also require the launching system of the missile defense to be stationed close to the area of the launch so that the anti-missiles could reach the missiles while they were still in the atmosphere. A boost-phase missile defense, if it were based on land or on ships, could not be close enough to a missile launch in countries the size of the Soviet Union, or China, although this objection would not apply to countries such as Iran or North Korea, which could be approached more closely. On the other hand, if the defensive rockets were deployed in planes, they would need to have already penetrated Soviet or Chinese airspace, which itself would be an act of war.

Were the missile defense system orbital, with satellites circling the earth approximately every ninety minutes, it would require an enormous number of satellites to ensure that one was close enough to hit the missile in the boost-phase. The cost of such a system would be prohibitive. If the defense system utilized energy or lasers directed from the air or from a satellite, it would encounter the problem of "thermal blooming," or the diffusion of energy as the energy beams hit the atmosphere. Because of these difficulties, no country has yet developed an effective "boost-phase" defense, although this defensive notion is still under development in the United States (see Chapter 4).

Halting a nuclear armed missile as it hones down upon its target at twenty times the speed of sound in the "terminal-phase" did not seem viable because if the missile actually hit, the explosion would rain destruction on the land being defended. Destroying a nuclear missile about to hit the United States by exploding it over U.S. territory was not an option. Even if a nuclear explosion were not triggered, carcinogenic plutonium would be scattered far and wide. (Ten pounds of plutonium is the trigger for a hydrogen bomb; less than one millionth of a gram of plutonium, if inhaled, is a carcinogenic dose.)

The most compelling option was to destroy the missile in

mid-course, after it left the atmosphere, as it transited outer space, and before it reentered the atmosphere close to its target. The first U.S. missile defense systems were designed to carry nuclear warheads. Such missiles would need only to get near Soviet nuclear warheads in space to destroy them, although these nuclear explosions, when they were actually tested, wreaked havoc in the upper atmosphere and in near space, causing great damage on the ground as well as destroying several of our own military satellites. Such explosions would also render outer space utterly unusable for communications, weather observation, information exchange, and other peaceful uses.

The testing of such weapons was ruled out in 1963 by the Limited Test Ban. A nuclear armed system was thus obviously unacceptable. The danger, however, that a country could pollute outer space through a nuclear blast continues, as a number of countries, including North Korea, which is not a party to the major weapons pacts, have the relatively cheap option of using a nuclear missile to destroy enemy satellites in wartime. Even more economically, the Chinese, with only a score of missiles pointed at the United States, the Soviets, or for that matter even the North Koreans in future scenarios could also prevent their bombs from being hit by U.S. anti-missiles by combining their bombs with decoys.

In current missile construction, the missile disgorges its "passengers" or nuclear weapons during the 25-minute transit time in outer space. The nuclear weapons then re-enter the earth's atmosphere to land independently on their targets. One missile can carry up to ten separate hydrogen bombs, which can be released together or separately. Prior to their release, or as the bombs are disgorged, they can be accompanied by milar balloons, decoys with the same shape and temperature as the warheads. To an anti-missile device, the decoys are indistinguishable from the warheads.

It would always be possible to overwhelm a defense system by launching thousands of incoming missiles simultaneously. But even if the number of missiles was small, the defense system could be overwhelmed by decoys, which could number up to a hundred per warhead. Because they will encounter no resistance in outer space, the balloons and warhead will travel at the same speed. If the decoys have the same shape and temperature as the warhead, the sensor system of any defense weapon designed to destroy these bombs will therefore be unable to discriminate between the decoys and the bombs. Technically easy to build and orders of magnitude cheaper than the warhead itself, these decoys could be used by any country with enough technical ability to mount a missile attack against the United States. After almost fifty years of research, the decoy problem remains unsolved, a fact unacknowledged by the U.S. government. The ultra-simplistic tests conducted on the U.S. ground-based system have never included the use of multiple decoys.[4]

At the "Full Spectrum Dominance" Conference in May 2005, Theodore Postol, one of the nation's top experts on missile defense, described the difficulties in dealing with decoys: "The big problem is not honing in on the warhead; the big problem is figuring out what's the warhead. . . . You have these targets, some are warheads, some are decoys, some are God knows what—what you are looking at is simply points of light. . . . We don't have a clue as to what the objects are." According to Postol, the warhead can't be distinguished from a balloon in outer space. "If it turns out the balloon is coated with the right material, it will look as bright as the warhead . . . this system has no hope of ever working. . . . I would submit that as a military scientist . . . this is a system that wouldn't make it off the drawing board if it weren't politicized beyond comprehension."

The more scientists and technicians have worked on a midcourse missile defense system, the less feasible it seems. Prototype systems have failed test after test, or have passed unrealistic or simplified tests, rendering the result meaningless. Occasionally, a test warhead has been shot down, but never one surrounded by groups of decoys, as they almost certainly would be in a real combat situation.

As scientists worked on missile defense research in the 1950s and

1960s, other potentially destabilizing collateral consequences became evident. Unless anti-missile weapons could be made to work with fairly comprehensive effectiveness, they would cause launching nations to build even more missiles in an attempt to beat the flawed defenses. Missile defense systems would also increase the military budget both directly through construction costs, and indirectly, because they would introduce the need to build more offensive missiles to compensate for missiles that might be shot down by the enemy. If the United States could build an anti-missile system, so too could the Soviets and the Chinese. The added missiles on both sides would, of course, also increase the extent of the mutual destruction and utter devastation if they were not knocked down by the missile defense systems. The crazy notion of missile defense would, ironically, generate ever more weapons, providing ever less security.

With all the options considered and found unworkable, the truth was inescapable. A missile defense system was simply not feasible for the foreseeable future. So in 1972, President Richard Nixon and Soviet leader Leonid Brezhnev agreed to the Anti-Ballistic Missile Treaty (the ABM Treaty), which eventually limited deployment of missile defenses to one site in each country, and which outlawed testing to create a national missile defense system.[5] The treaty prohibited the development, testing, and deployment of all types of anti-ballistic missile systems, including those in outer space.

Without missile defense, MAD became the only system keeping the United States and the USSR from destroying each other during the decades of the Cold War. Ironically, the ABM Treaty also helped by scaling down the number of missiles needed to make MAD work. Disarmament agreements, limiting the number of warheads and missiles on each side, further reduced the danger of a missile attack for several decades.

However, in the 1980s, missile defense reappeared on the American agenda when President Reagan proposed the Strategic Defense Initiative (SDI), designed to create an "astrodome" in the sky to protect the United States against the now huge Soviet long-range ballistic missile force which had been built in the intervening years. On March 23, 1983, President Reagan gave his famous "Star Wars" speech, disavowing MAD, and claiming that Republicans were the only party prepared to defend America, while Democrats endorsed ineffective arms control. Reagan began his speech by asking, "What if free people could live secure in the knowledge that their security did not rest upon the threat of instant retaliation to deter a Soviet attack, that we could intercept and destroy strategic ballistic missiles before they reached our own soil or that of our allies?" The president said he was directing "a long-term research and development program to begin to achieve our ultimate goal of eliminating the threat by strategic nuclear missiles."

Posters were spread throughout the country depicting President Reagan protecting the United States from a hail of incoming Soviet missiles with a missile defense dome covering the United States. But, in the tradition of their predecessors, Reagan-era scientists were also unable to create a system that worked. The SDI program, or "Star Wars," was initially based on kinetic "hit-to-kill" interceptors rather than the nuclear-tipped interceptors proposed in earlier systems. When this system did not work, scientist Edward Teller, best known as the "father of the H-bomb," and the Livermore Laboratory in California came up with a totally new idea that captured the imagination of the Reagan administration: the X-ray Laser.[6] The Reagan administration spent billions of dollars on the development of Teller's X-ray Laser. Advocates claimed that laser beams, propagated and energized by a nuclear explosion in outer space, could conceivably pick out and destroy all the Soviet incoming missiles. But almost from the beginning, a number of scientists, including MIT's Theodore Postol, understood that the system would not work and, in any case, was banned by the ABM Treaty, as well as the 1963 Limited Test Ban, prohibiting the testing of nuclear weapons in outer space.

The Soviets were clearly dubious about the effectiveness of the U.S. notion of missile defense. Strobe Talbott, in his book *Master of the Game*,[7] recorded the following conversation between President Reagan and Soviet leader Mikhail Gorbachev:

> The President said, "We are going forward with the research and development necessary to see if this is a workable concept and if it is, we are going to deploy it."
> Gorbachev answered, "Mr. President, you do what you think you have to do. . . . And if in the end you think you have a system you want to deploy, go ahead and deploy it. Who am I to tell you what to do? I think you're wasting money. I don't think it will work. But if that's what you want to do, go ahead."

In the end, although Teller vigorously promoted this idea for missile defense, it too proved unworkable. It is not clear whether Teller consciously deceived the president or simply failed to realize that his idea could not be technically realized. In any event, the efforts of Teller and the Livermore Laboratory to develop the X-ray Laser were quietly dropped in 1984, although the public was not informed for a number of years. Other systems under development during the Reagan period also failed to produce any assurance that even a majority of incoming missiles could be knocked out. So clear was it that missile defense systems wouldn't work that Soviet military spending during this period was flat or decreasing, despite claims that the threat of missile defense had spurred the Soviets to increased expenditures, and so had hastened their fall in 1989. Today, aspects of the failed X-ray Laser system are back on the drawing board as anti-satellite weapons.

In addition to Edward Teller, a lobbying group was also driving "Star Wars." Established in the 1960s, it comprised representatives of the arms industry, the Pentagon, development laboratories, and conservative think tanks. This formidable lobbying machinery is still in operation. Corporations such as Lockheed Martin, Boeing, Raytheon, Hughes Aircraft, TRW (subsequently acquired by Northrop Grumman), and others contributed substantial funds over the years to congressmen, and also gained their support by constructing missile plants in their congressional districts.

William D. Hartung, President's Fellow at the World Policy Institute and correspondent for *The Nation*, estimates that from 2001 to 2006, the top missile defense contractors donated more than $4.1 million dollars to thirty key members of Congress. He states that Lockheed Martin, Northrop Grumman, Boeing, SAIC, and General Dynamics made $13.1 million in campaign contributions between 2001 and 2006, and spent $30.2 million on lobbying in the year 2000 (the most recent year for which full data are available). The same companies that have been involved in missile defense are also actively pursuing the billions of dollars of contracts involved in space weaponization.[8]

As Alice Slater, president of the New York-based Global Resource Action Center for the Environment, points out, "Our government is being bribed by these corporations pushing for Star Wars. They have absolutely no regard for the safety and well-being of the world. This is almost a cliché about corporate greed—at a grand scale."[9] What all this means is that many decisions to develop and deploy missile defense systems and other space weapons are being made for political and economic rather than security reasons. This is why it is critical for citizens to ask questions and demand answers about many so-called military judgments.

Although George Bush Senior had disapproved of missile defense as vice president under Gerald Ford, during his 1988 presidential campaign the first President Bush supported full deployment and called for the ABM Treaty to be reinterpreted. Huge projected costs, however—over $250 billion—led him to abandon the idea of a comprehensive national missile defense system, and to advance a limited system, named "Global Protection Against Accidental Launch System (GPALS), instead.

Missile defense got a new spurt of energy when the then Secretary of Defense Richard Cheney falsely claimed that the U.S. Patriot anti-missiles successfully intercepted Scud missiles during the Gulf War in 1991, claims later largely negated by the General Accounting Office, which reported that Patriots hit only 9 percent of the Iraqi Scud warheads. The Israelis claimed that none had been hit. Televised footage believed by many Americans to have been tapes of Patriots intercepting actual Iraqi weapons turned out to be stock promotional footage of simulations and tests. Nevertheless, false and misleading claims for the success of the Patriot have continued to fuel support for missile defense. The somewhat better record of "theater" or short-range missile defenses during the 2003 Iraq War, and in recent testing, has also helped boost support for long-range missile defense. The problem is that range matters, particularly because incoming short- and middle-range missiles cannot use decoys, the major obstacle to defending against long-range missiles.

During the Reagan and Bush administrations, another anti-missile technology, also proposed by Edward Teller, drove a separate campaign for more appropriations. This was the idea of autonomous, small "kill-vehicles," which would be lifted into outer space to engage ICBMs in the boost-phase, as the missiles were launched. Called "Brilliant Pebbles," this system, like the X-ray Laser, consumed vast amounts of research money, and ultimately came to naught. Projected costs of $85 billion, poor performance, and the absurd growth in size of the "pebbles" into virtual "boulders" as more and more necessary equipment was added, doomed the project, and President Bush Senior eventually dropped it. By the end of the first Bush administration, around $100 billion had been spent on anti-missile research, making it the largest weapons-research project in history, with virtually nothing to show for it. Fourteen years later, "Brilliant

Pebbles" is under consideration again today, as the U.S. moves toward space weaponization (see Chapter 4).

In 1999, during the Clinton administration, the U.S. Senate, by a vote of 97–3, adopted legislation calling for deployment of national missile defense as soon as technologically possible. Nevertheless, on September 1, 2000, President Clinton announced that he would defer the decision to deploy such a system to the next administration, citing the system's unproven technology, dramatically brought home by a series of failed tests; the likelihood that countermeasures, such as decoys, could foil it; and the objections of Russia, China, and our NATO allies that deployment would jeopardize the 1972 ABM treaty. He also added four related caveats for any future funding: that the system be affordable, that it be technologically proven, that the missile threat be established, and that deployment not undermine the pursuit of arms control. Ironically, these same caveats, if taken seriously, would have prevented deployment of the present ground-based system installed by the current Bush administration, and plans for future deployment of a space-based system.

President George W. Bush ignored these problems and called for early deployment of a national missile defense system. Many of the same people and institutions that had lobbied successfully for a missile defense system in the earlier Reagan and Bush periods were back in the game. These included Donald Rumsfeld, Richard Perle, Paul Wolfowitz, and Frank Gaffney (who runs the Center for Security Policy), as well as the Heritage Foundation; and corporations such as Lockheed Martin, Boeing, Northrop Grumman, Raytheon, and General Dynamics, which have continued to donate millions of dollars to members of Congress to push through national missile defense.

One development that motivated President Bush was the 1998 report of the Commission to Assess the Ballistic Missile Threat headed by Donald Rumsfeld.[10] That report falsely claimed that, within a few years, North Korea, Iran, and Iraq, which President

Bush referred to as "rogue states," and the "axis of evil," could deploy operational intercontinental ballistic missile systems with "little or no warning," and that the United States could be threatened by such missiles as early as 2005. Not highlighted in the administration's argument for the immediate need to build a missile defense system in response was the fact that any long-range missile development by these countries would require an extended series of flight tests, which would allow the United States considerable warning time.

Moreover, because chemical weapons have only a limited effectiveness and microbes or spores would probably be destroyed on impact, only nuclear-armed ICBMs would be effective, and none of these countries possessed these. As Ambassador Thomas Graham, past director of the U.S. Arms Control and Disarmament Agency (ACDA) and President Clinton's special ambassador for nuclear disarmament, points out, "Developing a nuclear weapon small and light enough to be carried by a ballistic missile the considerable distance from, say, North Korea to the continental United States would also certainly require a series of nuclear weapon tests, which would provide additional warning."[11] Close analysis of the Rumsfeld report also reveals that Rumsfeld essentially changed the verbs of earlier less threatening CIA estimates from "mights" and "coulds" to "wills," a shift to a series of worst-case assumptions, despite the lack of evidence of any significant changes in other countries' real missile capability.[12] Nevertheless, the report cited an imminent threat as the rationale for the United States to begin immediate construction of a ballistic missile defense.

In 1999, a year after the report, the CIA concluded that over the next fifteen years the United States "most likely will face ICBM threats from Russia, China and North Korea, probably from Iran, and possibly from Iraq, although the threats will consist of dramatically fewer weapons than today because of significant reductions we expect in Russian strategic forces." The CIA report had, of course, dutifully reiterated some of the conclusions and techniques of the Rumsfeld report, supporting the case for deployment of a national missile defense.[13] A more balanced net assessment of global ballistic missile arsenals, undertaken by Joseph Cirincione of the Carnegie Endowment for International Peace, revealed that the ballistic-missile threat was confined, limited, and changing relatively slowly.[14]

Nevertheless, on December 13, 2001, President George W. Bush, marking the first abrogation of a disarmament treaty ever made by an American president, announced withdrawal from the ABM Treaty, which became effective in six months according to the terms of the treaty. The president stated, "Today, I have given formal notice to Russia, in accordance with the treaty, that the United States of America is withdrawing from this almost 30-year-old treaty. I have concluded the ABM Treaty hinders our government's ability to develop ways to protect our people from future terrorist or rogue state missile attacks." Thus was the door opened for the deployment of a national missile defense (NMD) system.

The president invoked terrorism to justify his withdrawal from the ABM Treaty, just as he would invoke terrorism to invade Iraq. But in neither case was terrorism really a factor. Given the enormous expense and technical difficulties involved in their development, intercontinental ballistic missiles are the least likely weapons for terrorists to acquire. Nor do terrorists have the capability to launch them. Weapons delivered by ships or planes, or hand-carried, or even cruise or short-ranged missiles, are much more likely weapons for terrorists, as the attacks of September 11 brought home. And these delivery systems will never be countered by national missile defense.[15]

Thirty-two congressmen, led by Representative Dennis Kucinich (D-OH), made a strong attempt to stop the president from withdrawing from the ABM Treaty of 1972 by suing him for illegal abrogation of the treaty without congressional consent.[16] The 2002 lawsuit requested that the federal courts make a decision about whether or not the Constitution permits the president to withdraw from a treaty without the consent of Congress. According to the suit, the Constitution states that treaties, once approved by the Senate and White House, are federal law and that the president does not enjoy the power to repeal federal laws without congressional approval.

At stake was not just the ABM Treaty, but all treaties to which the United States is presently signatory. If the president could withdraw from the ABM Treaty without congressional consent, the suit maintained, he could withdraw from any treaty to which the United States was a signatory: the United Nations, the Limited Test Ban of 1963, or the Non-Proliferation Pact of 1968. As Representative Kucinich stated, "The President's termination of the ABM treaty represents an unconstitutional repeal of a law duly enacted by Congress. If the President is allowed to repeal laws at his own instance, it would be destructive of our Constitution."

The president's withdrawal from the ABM Treaty had been cleverly timed. A little over a year after the September 11 attacks, with a limitless war against terrorism and the possibility of conflict with Iraq, President Bush relied on the well-developed convention that Congress does not oppose the president on strategic issues during wartime. Despite severe misgivings on the part of a number of U.S. senators on both sides of the aisle, no senator was willing to step up to the plate and join Representative Kucinich and his colleagues to become a co-plaintiff in the suit. On December 30, 2002, Justice John Bates of the District Court of Columbia, a Bush appointee, dismissed the lawsuit, stating that "issues concerning treaties are largely political questions best left to the political branches of the government, not the courts, for resolution." The lead attorney for the plaintiffs, Peter Weiss, concluded that the decision represented "a considerable advance toward the imperial presidency and a commensurate retreat from constitutional government."[17]

Unlike the modest plan that President Clinton had considered, which would develop land-based interceptors to knock down enemy warheads when the warhead was in space, President Bush wanted a far more complex missile defense program capable of intercepting warheads in all three phases of flight: boost, mid-course, and terminal. Subsequently, the United States announced plans to move ahead with an initial missile defense deployment at Fort Greeley, Alaska. The deployment in Alaska was declared to be directed toward North Korea, but the number of interceptors roughly matched the number of China's strategic missiles at the time. The present system being deployed at Fort Greeley and now additionally at Vandenberg Air Force Base in California, is based on mid-course interception and is expected to have up to thirty-eight interceptors by the end of 2009. Each defense missile will carry seven kill vehicles by as early as 2007, a development that is likely also to shape future space-based defenses.[18]

Even Pentagon officials have conceded, however, that the mid-course system being deployed in Alaska and California, which represents the largest initiative in the Bush system, has severe limitations. It can still be rendered inoperative by simple balloon decoys, similar to the kind sold in grocery stores, released from the missile as it transits outer space, or other countermeasures easily within the grasp of any country capable of launching a missile. Nevertheless, the largest single weapons expense in the U.S. defense budget for 2004 was the allocation of over $9 billion for missile defense; for 2007 that figure has risen to $10.4 billion.

In late 2006, North Korea unsuccessfully tested a very small nuclear device, thus joining the nuclear club, which now consists of the United States, Russia, China, United Kingdom, France, Israel, India, and Pakistan. However, North Korea has still not demonstrated the ability to launch an ICBM with a nuclear warhead, and it would be an act of national suicide for it to do so against the United States. Mid-course missile defense—a system that engages the warhead in outer space—even if it worked, which it does not, would not be the way of dealing with North Korea, but rather shorter-range missile defense, most likely launched from ships.[19] The installation of the mid-course defense system in Alaska and California, which cannot deal with decoys, seems to be essentially useless.

Despite this, a report from the Pentagon's testing office claims that the missile defense system "may have some inherent defensive capability to intercept North Korean missiles,"[20] but the Pentagon, according to Senator Carl Levin (D-MI) has been denying to the Senate the testing and evaluation data required by law. The system has been undertested, and many of the tests that have been made have been unsuccessful, relying for the most part on artificial elements that do not replicate battlefield conditions. Essentially, the tests are dumbed down, with targets and interceptor missiles often following a preprogrammed flight path to designated positions, and with single decoys at significantly different temperature and shape than the warhead to allow for easier identification. And no real attempt has been made to deal with the reality of decoys. Even Defense Department officials have acknowledged that tests are "carefully scripted."

To date, the United States has spent almost $150 billion on missile defense since President Dwight D. Eisenhower first proposed a modest program. The billions of dollars for long-range missile defense, which is a substantial part of this figure, have also necessarily limited defense spending in such critical areas as counter-terrorism and counter-proliferation of weapons of mass destruction, as well as underfunded aspects of homeland security, not to mention programs for the disadvantaged in the United States and abroad. If anything, these figures are likely to rise. According to the Congressional Budget Office, the annual cost of the current Bush administration's missile defense plans could almost double from $10.4 billion, the largest single program in the fiscal year 2007, to $19 billion by 2013, and total $247 billion from 2006 through fiscal 2024.[21]

Despite the president's rush to deployment, the Pentagon itself has raised serious doubts about the system. Thomas P. Christie, then Director of Operational Testing and Evaluations, declared on February 20, 2003, "One of my chief concerns is the potential for systems to circumvent the rigorous acquisition process and enter into full-rate production or into the hands of our warfighters without learning the operational capabilities and limitations demonstrated by adequate operational testing and evaluation." He questioned the readiness and adequacy of every major component of the missile system. Secretary of Defense Rumsfeld himself said on February 17, 2005, in answer to a question by Senator Hillary Clinton, "I agree . . . there is no deterrent if something is not known to work."[22]

As for a system that is more modest than President Reagan's Star Wars program, Rumsfeld smugly remarked, "To the extent we have a capability, it will have a deterrent effect. To the extent it has a limited capacity, it will have a deterrent effect only to that limit." Senator Levin countered, "What the Pentagon has tried not to emphasize is that this 'initial capacity' is likely to be marginally effective, if it works at all. Declaring this untested, marginal system ready to deploy is like declaring a newly designed airplane ready to fly before the wings have been attached to the airframe and the electronics installed in the cockpit." As a result, the United States will have the most expensive military development program in history, going full-steam-ahead with inadequate testing and virtually no congressional supervision.[23]

North Korea has been the country cited most frequently to justify the national missile defense system, and an expected North Korean missile launch proved the incentive to move the U.S. missile defense system from test mode to operational.[24] As early as 1999, the CIA in its National Intelligence Estimate indicated that North Korea had the capacity to create one or two nuclear weapons. Today it has the plutonium for six to eight bombs, and despite its nuclear test on October 9, 2006, it may not have developed a warhead small enough to fit on a missile.

On July 4, 2006, North Korea test-fired seven missiles over the Sea of Japan, including an intercontinental missile which either failed or was aborted. This missile, the Taepodong 2, could have hit Alaska or perhaps the West Coast of the United States, if it had worked. In the event that North Korea ever had the capacity to hit targets in the U.S. mainland, a *partially* effective missile defense system would be little consolation for America.[25] Far more effective in dissuading North Korea from launching an attack is, as we have indicated, the threat of nuclear retaliation, a threat that proved totally effective for decades during the Cold War against a far stronger opponent, and that seems already to have deterred North Korea from launching another attack on South Korea for over fifty years.

Ironically, President Bush initially focused on North Korea as the *raison d'être* for NMD at the very time that Pyongyang was moderating its policies, improving its relations with South Korea and Japan, and perhaps looking for ways to scale back its modest strategic programs. However, for almost five years, the Bush administration refused to conduct meaningful negotiations with North Korea. The ambassador in charge was John Bolton, now the U.S. ambassador to the United Nations, whose behavior illustrates his belief that diplomacy should be conducted primarily through bluster and insult.

Now that Bolton is no longer the negotiator in North Korea, diplomacy may be tried again with Assistant Secretary of State Christopher R. Hill as the U.S. spokesperson, even after North Korea's nuclear test. With the administration pursuing bilateral discussion with North Korea in the context of the six-power talks (Russia, China, North and South Korea, Japan, and the United States), some progress could be made. North Korea is currently insisting on being able to develop nuclear fuel for reactors, as it was allowed to do under the 1968 Nuclear Non-Proliferation Treaty, from which it withdrew in 2003. However, such fuel can also be used to create additional nuclear weapons, and the North Koreans' intentions remain unclear. Despite this problem, and the fact that America's still tentative interest in negotiation comes five years late, negotiations still hold the promise of solving the North Korean problem.[26]

Ironically, on July 9, 2006, India test-fired a missile with a reputed range of 1,800 miles, which would put a number of Chinese cities within striking distance. While unsuccessful, the launch occurred at the time that India is negotiating a pact with the United States whereby the United States would aid the Indian civilian nuclear program, freeing up limited supplies for India's military nuclear program. In contrast to North Korea, the United States registered no protest concerning the Indian launch.[27] India, like North Korea, also does not belong to the Nuclear Non-Proliferation Treaty.

The other troubling case is Iran, which insists on its right to enrich uranium, a right which it enjoys under the Nuclear Non-Proliferation Treaty. But once a country can enrich uranium in low concentration for nuclear reactor fuel, it can then enrich it to high concentration suitable for nuclear weapons. In July 2000, Iran completed its first successful test of a medium-range missile (there is no treaty to prevent such testing). With this capacity, Iran could not threaten the U.S. homeland but it could hit key targets in the Middle East, including Saudi Arabia, Turkey, and Israel. Meaningfully in this context, the president of Iran, Mahmoud Amedinejad, has recently made threats denying the very right of Israel to exist. Iran's ability to hit targets in the Middle East could convince the United States not to attack Iran.[28] Here, both Israel's and the United States's greater success with theater missile defenses (short-range missiles, not missiles in outer space) could offer some help. As reported by UPI's Martin Sieff, "Senior Israeli defense officials are publicly proclaiming the reliability of their Arrow anti-ballistic missile interceptor in what appears to be a clear deterrence warning to Iran not to try and launch any nuclear missile strike against the Jewish state." A high-ranking Israel Defense Forces officer told the *Jerusalem Post*, "We will shoot all of Iran's missiles down."[29]

Meanwhile, U.S. Senate Majority Leader Bill Frist had been urging President Bush to step up efforts to put an interceptor missile site in Europe to protect against potential attacks from Iran. Senator Frist said in a letter, "As Iran continues to make progress in deploying its Shahab 3 missiles and developing new, longer range missiles, while simultaneously pursuing nuclear weapons, the ability to shoot down Iranian warheads in flight becomes increasingly critical to our national security" (although according to the IAEA there is no evidence that Iran is intent on making nuclear weapons).[30] Currently, the United States is seeking to have ten anti-missile interceptors in Europe by 2011, with the most likely site being Poland or the Czech Republic. Such a site in Poland would be the first permanent U.S. military presence in that country, a move that might well be taken as threatening by Russia.[31]

In April of 2006, the United States was suggesting the possibility of a preemptive strike on Iran. Dr. Kurt Gottfried, Chairman of the Union of Concerned Scientists, stated: "Recent reports suggest that the Bush administration is considering using nuclear weapons against Iran. The very fact that nuclear weapon use is being discussed as an option against a state that does not have nuclear weapons and does not represent a direct or imminent threat to the United States illustrates the extent to which the Bush administration has changed U.S. nuclear weapons policy."[32] By invading Iraq and militarily threatening Iran, the president has provided every motive for Iran to keep its conservative government and to develop a nuclear deterrent and a missile system capable of delivering it. As a member of the Bush-designated "axis of evil," Iran has played out the part that the Bush administration scripted for it.

The deployment of missile defense has been represented by the current U.S. administration as designed to deter an attack by North

Korea, or even possibly Iran, although neither country has the capacity to hit the United States. But even if Iran or North Korea should achieve long-range missile capacity, a missile attack is unlikely because a missile always carries a return address, and the United States maintains the ability to obliterate either country. Such an attack would simply be an act of national suicide.

If the United States did preemtively attack North Korea or Iran, it could destroy their missile forces before they had a chance to launch. If this proved unsuccessful, and North Korea or Iran were able to launch missiles, the U.S. missile defense system would attempt to neutralize the missiles before they could hit their targets. Missile defense would then be part of the total attack system, and it is clear that North Korea and Iran regard the U.S. missile defense system in this light as an offensive rather than a defensive system.[33]

Most likely, despite public statements to the contrary, the main target of U.S. missile defense development has been China, which does have the present capacity to hit the United States with ICBMs. China, which reputedly has about twenty ICBMs pointed at the United States, has made clear that, were the United States to create a missile defense system, the Chinese would simply increase their number of ICBMs so that it could continue to maintain nuclear deterrence in the face of what it considers to be continual American threats.[34] As Ambassador Thomas Graham points out, China will simply compensate, and perhaps overcompensate, for any missile defense system we employ. He states that "the Chinese would 'worst case' our system and decide that their nuclear forces are threatened with being nullified, causing them to significantly increase the size of their long-range nuclear missile force—up to ten times, in their own words—thereby worsening the threat to the United States."[35] A national missile defense system would be useless against scores or hundreds of Chinese nuclear-armed missiles winging their way toward U.S. cities. War games played against China, threatening comments in defense policy statements, aggressive encounters over currency, and trade questions have stoked up the possibility of a future encounter. But the kind of missile defense we are deploying does not provide the United States adequate security even now against Chinese ICBMs. Rather than continue inadequate missile defenses along with U.S. aggressive posturing with the Chinese, it makes far more sense to deal with this country now on a diplomatic basis.

Despite a string of test failures, and earlier indications that the program might be curtailed, the deployment of missile defenses in Alaska and California continues, and is being expanded. To shield the government from continuing criticism, the testing is being increasingly classified and restricted. It would appear that Senator Ted Stevens, Republican from Alaska, has successfully defended the missile system, despite the fact that it doesn't work; a clearer example of pork-barreling could hardly be found.

President Bush has banked on the fact that the American people support missile defense, if it works. A poll in March of 2006 indicated that "More than 70 percent of citizens throughout the state of New York support a missile defense system with the ability to protect the United States from a nuclear, chemical or biological attack." The question is, of course, does it work?[36]

To date, however, the military has not declared the system operational, and has even suggested that it might never be.[37] As an alternative, the Missile Defense Agency continues to pursue boost-phase defenses, and is experimenting with the idea of orbiting satellites in outer space which will directly ram into the opposing missiles. Called "kinetic kill vehicles," this defense system, like boost-phase defenses, is fraught with enormous problems, and is perhaps even less feasible than the failed ground-based system in Alaska and California (see Chapter 4).

Meanwhile, however, the system that employs sensors to track and collide with a missile in space might, with only small modifications, be used to knock out satellites, and is now forming the technical basis for anti-satellite warfare. As the Bush administration moves toward space weaponization, and toward extending missile defense from earth-based to space-based, it is important that the administration's history of deceit in claiming the need for long-range missile defense and of deploying a system that doesn't work be kept clearly in mind. How much longer should this charade be allowed to go on before the United States puts its money and effort into more feasible measures of securing the heavens, including multilateral diplomacy? Instead, it is moving in exactly the opposite direction: toward the weaponization of outer space.

4

The Weaponization of Outer Space

To the arrogant I say, "Boast no more,"
and to the wicked, "Do not lift up your horns.
Do not lift your horns against heaven;
do not speak with outstretched neck.

—Psalm 75: 4–5

Force application by kinetic kill weapons will enable
pinpoint strikes on targets anywhere in the world. The
equivalent of the Desert Storm strategic air campaign
against Iraq infrastructure would be possible to com-
plete in minutes to hours essentially on immediate no-
tice.

—U.S. Air Force Advisory Board[1]

The concept of the militarization of outer space developed simultaneously to, and as an outgrowth of, missile defense. The central strategy of Full Spectrum Dominance upon which space weapons are predicated emerged less than ten years ago in a 1997 policy paper titled "Vision for 2020," produced by the U.S. Space Command. The paper declared that

over the past several decades, space power has primarily supported land, sea, and air operations—strategically and operationally. During the early portion of the twenty-first century, space power will also evolve into a separate and equal medium of warfare. Likewise, space forces will emerge to protect military and commercial national interests and investment in the space medium due to their increasing importance. . . . The emerging synergy of space superiority with land, sea, and air superiority, will lead to Full Spectrum Dominance. . . . As space systems become lucrative military targets, there will be a critical need to control the space medium to ensure U.S. dominance on future battlefields. Robust capabilities to ensure space superiority must be developed—just as they have been for land, sea, and air.[2]

The idea of controlling or dominating outer space is not new. It first appeared in the United States at the very beginning of the space age, even before the United States launched its first satellite. In February of 1958, at the national conference of the Air Force Association, Thomas Dresser White, Chief of Staff of the Air Force, spelled out an early version of the concept: "The United States must win and maintain the capability to control space in order to assure the progress and preeminence of the free nations. If liberty and freedom are to remain in the world, the United States and its allies must be in a position to control space. We cannot permit the dominance of space to those who have repeatedly stated they intend to crush the free world." White went on to clarify his objectives, however: "You will note that I stated the United States must win and maintain the capability to control space. I did not say that we should control space. There is an important distinction here. We want all nations to join with us in such measures as are necessary to ensure that outer space shall never be used for any but peaceful purposes."[3]

This clarification was lost in the decades which followed White's speech. The idea of dominating space, however, was expressed repeatedly in the first years of the U.S. space program, while the perceived military advantages of outer space competed with the peaceful uses of outer space and the prospects of international cooperation across a wide spectrum of uses. Indeed, the United States became preoccupied with the military uses of outer space, and the need for control.

In the following decades, the military opportunities posed by outer space began to create a mind-set that regarded space as a battlefield. Warfare in outer space was considered not as a possibility to be avoided, but a likely contingency to prepare for. As Michael Moore, contributing editor to *The Bulletin of the Atomic Scientists*, points out, "The men and women I call space warriors are part of a professional belief community whose members share certain overarching paradigms—one being that conflict in space is probable if not inevitable and the United States must therefore prepare for it by taking unilateral action that would give the United States control of space in time of conflict."[4] This belief was shared not only by military planners, whose power was directly tied up in the use of space for military purposes, but by a segment of the U.S. Congress that was a direct beneficiary of the space lobby, from whom they consistently received significant campaign contributions and help. This group has continued without substantial break for over fifty years to influence U.S. policy in the direction of Full Spectrum Dominance, and today, space weaponization.

Not just venality, however, motivates this group. Full Spectrum Dominance is also a form of psychic inflation, greed for power. Rather than a cooperative state in the multilateral context of a globalized world, the United States will be the supreme superpower, setting policy, fighting preemptive wars, dominating land, sea, air, and outer space. Despite the huge resources which the United States commands, it is a policy that puts these resources to tests they cannot pass, as exemplified by Iraq. Yes, the United States could invade Iraq, but could it simultaneously invade a score of other countries? Was not the first test of this doctrine of unilateral power flunked decisively?

During the Cold War outer space was only marginally employed in the service of ground-based weapons. The United States continued to employ military satellites for spying and target identification, and ballistic missiles employed flight paths that traversed outer space. Although the United States conducted a limited number of tests involving anti-satellites, space was never fully exploited as a battlefield or a staging area for weapons. Indeed, it was clear to many that outer space was more valuable in keeping the peace than in fighting wars. Satellites were used both for checking on enemy missile forces and for monitoring the growing number of arms control treaties. With huge expenditures maintaining the Cold War level of armaments, the defense industry hardly needed another market for its nefarious wares. The end of the Cold War also marked the severe shrinkage of the arms market, however. It is not a coincidence that within a decade of the fall of the Berlin Wall, the Space Command's "Vision for 2020" was issued.[5]

The new policy was further defined in January 2001 under the second Bush administration by a report of the Commission to Assess United States National Security Space Management and Organization, which had been set up by the Republican Congress in 1999, with Bob Smith (R-NH) serving as point person. The commission was chaired by Donald Rumsfeld before his subsequent appointment as Secretary of Defense by President Bush. The 2001 report concluded:

> If the U.S. is to avoid a space Pearl Harbor, it needs to take seriously the possibility of an attack on U.S. space systems. . . . Those hostile to the U.S. can acquire on the global market the means to deny, disrupt or destroy U.S. space systems by attacking satellites in space, communications links to and from the ground or ground stations that command the satellites and process their data.
>
> The Commissioners believe that the U.S. government should vigorously pursue the capabilities called for in the National Space Policy to ensure that the President will have the option to deploy weapons in space to deter threats to and, if necessary, defend against attacks on U.S. interests.

In order to extend its deterrence concepts and capabilities to space, the U.S. will require development of new military capabilities for operation to, from, in and through space.[6]

In August 2004, the U.S. Air Force moved even further toward space weaponization with the release of its Counterspace Operations doctrine. This document explicitly mentions military operations conceived to "deceive, disrupt, deny, degrade, or destroy adversary space capabilities."[7] The belligerent tone of these recent pronouncements is as disturbing as their content. They employ rhetoric of complete dominance and hegemony, not multilateral cooperation or diplomacy. Yet with these proclamations, the way has been cleared for the weaponization of outer space.

The notion of a "space Pearl Harbor" borders on the absurd, because other nations fully realize that an attack on U.S. space assets would necessarily involve their own nuclear annihilation. When the Japanese attacked the American fleet on December 7, 1941, there were no atomic bombs, and the United States was not mobilized to fight a war. Karl Mueller, political scientist at the RAND Corporation, says that the Rumsfeld Commission's conclusion that space warfare is inevitable was "based on a smattering of evidence and logic, extrapolated into facile overgeneralizations that are well-suited for television talk-show punditry but which are a poor basis for national policymaking."[8] Yet, it is precisely this kind of warped thinking that is steering the United States into space weapons.

In recent years, the United States has taken the first steps toward its stated goal of Full Spectrum Dominance. On May 18, 2005, Tim Weiner of the New York Times, noted: "With little public debate, the Pentagon has already spent billions of dollars developing space weapons and preparing plans to deploy them." Weiner cited recent statements by Pentagon officials affirming this policy:

- From Pete Teets, who recently stepped down as the acting Secretary of the Air Force: "We haven't reached the point of strafing and bombing from space. Nevertheless, we are thinking about such policies."
- From General Lance Lord, who heads the Air Force Space Command: "We must establish and maintain space superiority. Simply put, it's the American way of fighting."
- From General James E. Cartwright, who heads the United States Strategic Command, who told the Senate Armed Services nuclear forces subcommittee that the aim of developing space weaponry was to allow the nation to deliver an attack "very quickly, with very short time lines on the planning and delivery, any place on the face of the earth."[9]

While, as we have seen, the placement of satellites in space can yield immense benefits to mankind, the growing dependence of the United States and other countries on outer space military and commercial systems has been deemed to require the weaponization of space to protect these assets. During the Cold War, both the Soviet Union and the United States developed military space systems to provide warning of nuclear attack. Nuclear attacks could be discerned from a satellite which detected the launch plume of a missile, and nuclear testing could be identified by the particular thermal signal of a nuclear detonation. Satellites were also developed to provide military communications, reconnaissance, and intelligence, as well as the guidance of weapons. Satellite imagery is so sharp and finely tuned today that pictures can identify tiny ground-based objects of 15 centimeters' width, while infrared sensors and space-based radar can provide pictures with less than a meter of resolution.[10] During its recent wars in the Middle East, the United States further demonstrated its dependence on satellites, for communication, target identification, and for weapons guidance. But protection of these tremendously sophisticated satellites has led to the development of equally sophisticated weaponry to protect them—mostly designed to be based in space. These include counter-jamming devices, shielding against blasts and radiation, and "redundancy"—the deployment of more satellites than necessary to insure against loss. Weapons have also been developed to protect the ground stations from which such missiles are launched.

Apart from these defensive measures, dependence by the United States on satellite-directed warfare has led to its development of aggressive means to destroy or counter the space capacity of other countries. In moving toward such weapons, the United States is particularly concerned with China, as exemplified by numerous hostile statements in Department of Defense documents, in war games with the Chinese as the putative enemy, and in direct actions to control outer space.

While the United States has moved to perfect its use of satellites for military reconnaissance and fire direction control, it has also moved into outer space with another set of weapons: missile defense. Today, the United States is conducting basic research on the Space-Based Laser (SBL), which would operate in low-earth orbit and destroy hostile ballistic missiles during their boost-phase. While it might be argued that the Bush administration is moving into outer space as an alternative to its failed ground-based system, it is still doubtful that the administration accepts its ground-based midcourse defense as a definite and final failure. Rather, it has been pushing space-based defense not as a substitute for ground-based defense, but as part of its concept of a multilayered defense, which also includes sea-based interceptors that are carried on the U.S. Navy's Aegis ships and the Terminal High-Altitude Area Defense (THAAD), systems designed for short- and medium-range missiles.

The deployment in Alaska and California is only part of the package, and is not intended itself to be a full-fledged national missile defense system. Paul Wolfowitz, then U.S. Deputy Defense Secretary, and one of the major figures in the Bush foreign policy group, declared in 2001, "It is not an effort to build an impenetrable shield around the U.S. This is not Star Wars [when President Reagan spoke of a comprehensive missile defense shield]. We have a much more limited objective to deploy effective defenses against limited missile attack."[11]

Now, despite Wolfowitz's placating words, the United States is considering the possibility of a comprehensive missile defense, with at least one major component in outer space. Here, as in its ground-based defense, the United States is proceeding despite technical difficulties, and a rash of negative reports by the Government Accountability Office (GAO) on the ground-based system, which should create a sense of caution in moving ahead with space-based defenses. The reports not only deal with launch failures, but also poor planning, unmet schedules, inadequate security, problems with quality control, and cost overruns. A January 2006 report states, "[I]f, however, costs grow as they have historically, pursuing the programs included in CBO's missile defense projection will cost an additional $3 billion a year, on average, peaking at about $19 billion in 2013."[12]

The Space-Based Laser, for example, has still not overcome a basic problem with using directed energy in the atmosphere—the phenomenon called "thermal blooming" in which the energy spreads in the atmosphere and so loses its power. Another problem is that the satellite needs to be very close to the target, which means having a huge number of satellites in orbit so that one might be in the proper location at the time of the missile's launch.[13] However, if the U.S. history of missile defense is any clue, these problems will not inhibit development or deployment. The problem of decoys in mid-course missile defense was never solved, yet the system went into deployment, consuming tens of billions of U.S. taxpayer dollars. As some at the Pentagon say, this is a policy of "buy before you fly." As late as February 2006, a missile defense war game played on Capitol Hill did not use decoys, and as Representative Rush Holt (D-NY) noted, "The values used in the stimulation are not based on real data. . . . This should give you considerable skepticism about what these simulations may be showing about actual defense capabilities."[14]

In addition, according to Lt. Gen. Trey Obering, the Missile Defense Agency's director, the agency plans in 2008 to begin experiments in space to test the viability of placing anti-missile interceptors in orbit. One program, called the Space-Based Interceptor Test Bed, would launch up to five satellites capable of shooting down missiles. Another, for which the agency has asked Congress for $220 million to develop, is called "Multiple Kill Vehicles."[15]

Jeremy Singer, of *Space News*, reports: "The U.S. Missile Defense Agency (MDA) intends to spend nearly $675 million from 2008 through 2011 to develop an experimental constellation of space-based missile interceptors that would launch in 2012, according to budget justification documents submitted to Congress in March [of 2005]." The satellites in this system would destroy their targets through kinetic contact, that is, by ramming them with the extraordinary speeds possible in low-earth orbit. But this scheme would create masses of orbital debris, either by testing the system, or by actual deployment. Singer estimates that by 2016, there will be 50 to 100 such interceptors.[16]

Still another system, the Evolutionary Air and Space Global Laser Engagement, or Eagle, project will put mirrors underneath a huge airship, reputedly twenty-five times the size of the Goodyear blimp. Lasers, fired from the ground, the air, or from space, would bounce off these blimp-borne mirrors to track or destroy enemy missiles.[17] Some components that could assist these systems are presently being developed and will be deployed almost immediately. The Space-Based Infrared System (SBIS), which will be used to guide all ballistic missile defense interceptors—boost-phase, mid-course, and terminal-phase, will be first launched in 2006, and the full constellation of about thirty satellites could be in orbit by 2011, although it is presently being delayed.[18] Once installed, the system would use satellites in low-earth and geosynchronous orbits. The SBIS will also provide warning of missile launches and greatly expand capabilities for intelligence, surveillance, and reconnaissance missions. This will be a key component to space-based missile defense. Once it is in operation, it could be quickly followed by a deployable missile defense system.

Finally, the Space Tracking and Surveillance System (STSS) will be a constellation of low-earth orbit sensor satellites that will track enemy missiles, discriminate between warheads and decoys, and assess the outcome of possible interceptions. A test of two demonstration satellites is scheduled for 2007, although the Council for a Livable World estimates that deployment "is obviously well into the indefinite future."[19]

Theresa Hitchens of the Center for Defense Information indicates a considerable amount of deception in the decision to create an outer space component of the missile defense program. She writes that "the budget documents make very clear that MDA has already made a decision to field a space-based missile defense layer, contrary to what MDA officials have been saying in public about not 'making a decision' until 2008." Last year, she reports, MDA described the system as including 50 to 100 interceptors for both boost-phase and mid-course defenses. It is also engaged in a number of developmental projects upon which the Space-Based Test Bed will be constructed.[20]

In 2002, at the time of the U.S. withdrawal from the Anti-Ballistic Missile (ABM) Treaty, the Russian delegation to the Non-Proliferation Committee prophetically stated that "the withdrawal from the ABM Treaty may bring along such a dangerous development of events as 'weaponization' of space."[21] A direct effect of U.S. withdrawal from the ABM Treaty, in addition to the development of missile defense systems, both on the ground and in outer space, has been the development of anti-satellite capacity, using much of the technology that it developed for anti-missile defenses. The

ABM Treaty required both the United States and the Soviet Union to refrain from interference with "national technical means of verification," or spy satellites, which were a mechanism for stabilizing the relationship of the United States and the Soviet Union during the Cold War. Although the 1972 Strategic Arms Limitation Talks (SALT) also has such a provision, the end of the ABM Treaty has clearly weakened global stability by making such satellites targets.

As the United States moves toward space-based anti-missile systems, it is proceeding toward a major investment in an unproven form of defense, and one which, for many cogent reasons, should not be undertaken at all. The cost of an effective space-based system that could protect the country against an attack by a relatively small number of missiles has been estimated as anywhere from $220 billion to $1 trillion dollars.[22] Spending this exorbitant amount of money on an unnecessary and unproven system, at a time when the United States is experiencing $400 billion annual deficits, huge trade imbalances, and is radically cutting benefits to students, the elderly, and the poor, brings into question both our values and our judgment.

So far the United States has used space to launch its ICBMs and ground-based missile defenses, and orbit satellites to spot targets on the ground and direct its weapons. Now the United States is moving beyond these uses to dominate outer space by destroying the space capacity of other nations, either from the ground or from outer space. It is also planning to orbit weapons which will directly attack the satellites of other countries, and bombard targets on the earth.

The first part of this aggressive scenario is to attack satellites in orbit by jamming their signals and interrupting or distorting their radio communications; hence the United States is working to develop sophisticated jamming equipment, either from its ground stations or from the satellites themselves. The methods of doing this have been in development since the 1950s, but have become

increasingly effective. Jamming can involve disrupting communication by using a signal at the same frequency or higher power. In
"spoofing," the receiver is given a usable but false signal. If the satellites are sending back information on targets, the information will
be gutted; if the ground station is signaling the satellite to fire a
weapon, this can be stopped; if it is telling it to interfere with the
satellite of another country, this can be obstructed. However, jamming cannot be conducted without the target nation knowing its
satellites are under attack by picking up an interference signal, or by
sensing that communication with the satellite has been lost. While
the United States has perfected its jamming operations, it is not alone
in having this technology. It is readily available, and points up the
vulnerability of satellites to interference by other nations. The fact,
for instance, that Iraq, a country considerably less advanced than
many, acquired equipment to jam the U.S. GPS-guided munitions
during the recent Iraq War indicates that jamming capacity is spread-
ing, and is fairly widely accessible.[23]

Another method of destroying a rival nation's space power is
to attack the enemy's outer space ground stations and its communication links by using conventional ground-based missiles, airplanes,
or satellites from outer space. Here, ICBMs can be employed, just
as they were during the Cold War, to target an enemy's launching
stations on the ground. The same kind of missile attacks can be
conducted by airplane, by missiles guided by orbiting satellites, or
missiles launched directly from outer space. As the United States
moves toward direct space weaponization, it will be exploiting this
latter option. Today, all space powers are working on the means to
physically resist explosions that may damage their satellites and to
maintain communications during an attack while at the same time
working to attack their rivals.

In addition to using lasers to destroy satellites or ground
bases,[24] lasers can be designed to swamp a satellite's optical sensor
by light which is brighter than the light reflected from the target

that it is attempting to image. This technique is called "dazzling." Such a technique would be used to render inoperative satellites taking ground pictures of American bases or launch facilities.[25] Another directed energy weapon under consideration is a device that produces high-power microwaves, that is, waves shorter than radio waves but longer than visible light waves. These are the waves used by radars. If sent from the ground, such waves would be disrupted by the atmosphere; for this reason, they are being considered for use from satellites. Such weapons could disrupt or damage a rival's satellite's electronic system.[26]

Today, the United States is the world leader in developing these "star-wars" technologies to negate space systems by interfering with satellite communications.[27] These techniques are designed mainly to be used against satellites in geosynchronous orbit, which are otherwise fairly immune to physical threats from lower-earth orbit satellites or from missiles.

Attacks that damage or destroy satellites through direct contact with another object are called "kinetic energy" attacks. If the attack comes from the ground, the "kill vehicle" needs a homing device to locate its target. It might also release a cloud of pellets that would increase the likelihood of the target being hit. Because the speed of objects in space is so enormous—up to 17,000 miles an hour—small pellets can do major damage. The United States successfully tested such an interceptor against a low-earth orbit satellite in the early 1980s, and has been developing them ever since. An attack of this kind can be launched from the ground, or can be launched from satellites already in orbit.

Another important trend is the development of microsatellites—less than 500 kilograms as compared to several thousand kilograms for most satellites—which are cheaper, require smaller launch vehicles, and are harder to detect. Tim Weiner of the *New York Times* reported that the Air Force, in April of 2005, "launched the XSS-11, an experimental microsatellite with the technical ability to disrupt other nations' military reconnaissance and communications satellites." When deployed, the XSS-11 is expected to rendezvous with up to eight objects, and holds the possibility of being a full-fledged anti-satellite."[28] Microsatellites can be used as anti-satellite weapons, as inspectors of satellites in orbit to report on their purpose, or as space mines. Both the United States and China have indicated that they could launch microsatellites from larger satellites, although the Chinese capability is not verified.[29]

These programs use much of the technology that was developed for the ground-based anti-missile program, currently deployed in Alaska and California, because it is only a short step from hitting a missile in outer space to hitting an orbiting satellite. Space-based weapons are particularly vulnerable to such attacks. The Near Field Infra Red Experiment, called the NFIRE satellite, would track and kill missiles, and is only a year away from testing. To be fully effective to cover just the latitudes of Iran and North Korea, such a system would cost over $44 billion. Because of protests in Congress, initial NFIRE tests will not include the kill vehicle. Another system, the Kinetic Energy Anti-Satellite Weapon (KE-ASAT), is being considered to launch projectiles from earth capable of destroying satellites in orbit.[30]

Obviously if NFIRE and other such systems are deployed, they will provoke countermeasures by powers such as China and Russia. On April 9, 2000, an editorial in the *Moscow Times* stated:

> NFIRE is itself weaponized, carrying a projectile-packed "kill vehicle" that can destroy passing missiles—or the satellites of the United States' military and commercial rivals, as ABC News reported last week. This marks the first time in history that any nation has put a weapon in space, despite America's still-official policy against such a practice. And as Pentagon officials made clear in an eye-opening presentation to Congress in February, NFIRE's test is just

the first spark of a conflagration that will soon set the heavens ablaze with American weaponry capable of striking—and destroying—any spot on earth. As one top Pentagon official—opposed to this lunatic proliferation, thus remaining anonymous—said: "We're crossing the Rubicon into space weaponization."

High-altitude nuclear detonations are effective methods of destroying satellites and are within the capacity of all nuclear-capable states, although, for the United States, perhaps the least likely method that would necessarily be considered. Such an explosion would cause immediate damage to satellites, and could create a radiation belt that impacts upon most satellites in low-earth orbit. Many countries, such as China, India, Pakistan, Israel, Japan, Russia, and the United States, as well as the European Union, are capable of putting a nuclear warhead into outer space.[31] The United States and other space-launching nations are already shielding their satellites from the effects of such nuclear blasts. They are also, to the extent possible, placing their military satellites in higher and less vulnerable orbits.

A whole range of supporting technologies is presently underway for the development of anti-satellite weapons. These include: the capacity for precision maneuverability, large acceleration for the final stages of honing in on the satellite under attack, accurate global positioning capabilities, high-powered lasers, microsatellites, and precision reentry technology. Many of these technologies do not appear in the military budgets under specific weapon designations, so that a significant portion of the money used for anti-satellite and strike-based weapons is difficult to trace.

As the United States moves toward full deployment of space-based weapon satellites, other nations are developing the means to disrupt them or knock them down. Space-based weapon satellites are vulnerable. As Michael Krepon of the Stimson Center points out, "Defensive measures can make attacks on satellites more difficult, more expensive, more obvious, and less consequential, but they cannot ensure survivability under attack." According to Krepon,

> deterrence does not require dedicated ASATs or flight tests and deployments of space weapons, since it is well understood that weapons systems designed for other purposes have the inherent capability to disrupt or destroy satellites. Indeed, these residual capabilities are growing, as the United States pursues advanced missile defenses and the airborne laser program that are designed for other missions but that could, if needed, be utilized against the satellites of a state that initiates space warfare.

Thus, he concludes, "The United States does not need to flight-test and deploy space weapons, whether offense or 'defensive' in nature."[32]

A whole other category of space-based weapons under development is known as space force applications. These weapons essentially rely on gravity and complex navigational features to strike locations on earth with weapons based in outer space. While billions of research dollars have been spent on designs for such weapons, no such weapon has yet been deployed, although deployment may come within the next decade unless Congress acts to stop it.[33] Official statements by the U.S. government make clear that this is a real possibility. For example, the "Strategic Master Plan FY06 and Beyond" of the Air Force Space Command states, "Planners should consider integrating future development capabilities, such as the capability to deliver attacks from space, into the campaign plan when determining how best to strike adversary Centers of Gravity (COG). Space force application systems would have the advantage of rapid global access and the ability to effectively bypass adversary defenses."

Will such weapons be deployed? Money spent on development creates momentum for testing and deployment, and even if the weapons are imperfect, the model that the United States used in missile defense is to deploy a system which is known not to work and then try to improve it, rather than determine in advance whether a system is in fact operational.

Although space-based weapons are in sync with the sense of hegemonic power being promoted by the Bush administration, ground-based weapons are much cheaper, and for the most part, far more effective in military engagements than virtually anything the United States has on the drawing board for outer space. Dr. David Wright, Co-Director and Senior Scientist, Global Security Program, Union of Concerned Scientists, makes clear that outer space is a poor area from which to launch attacks on the ground, sea, or air. Nor is it optimal for creating platforms to combat missiles or deny the use of space to other countries.[34] While using outer space swells the ego of space planners, it impoverishes the nation, and does little or nothing for U.S. security.

One major space force application plan under development is the "Global Strike" program, which projects a 30-minute response time to drop sensors or bombs anywhere on the earth's surface from outer space. The Global Strike program is designed to employ military satellites capable of carrying about 500 kilograms of high-precision weapons to strike enemy military bases and command and control facilities. This program would require the placement of one hundred satellites in low-earth orbit, which would be many times more expensive than the use of ground-based missiles.[35]

Another Air Force–initiated strategy calls for a military space plane armed with precision-weapons with a half-ton of munitions, which could destroy command centers or missile bases anywhere in the world within 45 minutes. The Common Aero Vehicle (CAV) will be tested in 2006. It is an unmanned maneuverable spacecraft that will travel at five times the speed of sound and can carry a 12,000-pound payload comprising several hypersonic vehicles. Each of these vehicles will carry approximately 1,000 pounds of munitions or intelligence sensors. The first generation of these weapons is planned for 2010. CAVs, unlike missiles, can be recalled, and so they can be launched toward a potential target even before a final decision is made to attack. They would also obviate the need for nearby air bases. General Lance W. Lord, Commander of the Air Force Space Command, stated to the House Armed Services Committee in 2005: "This [CAV] is an incredible capability to provide the war fighter with a global reach capability against high payoff targets. . . . This is the type of Prompt Global Strike I have identified as a top priority for our space and missile force."[36]

Yet another "brilliant" space weapon on the drawing board is the long-rod penetrator, or "Rods from God." This system would dispatch 20-foot-long orbital tungsten or uranium rods that would enter the earth's atmosphere using the accelerating force of gravity to attack ground targets at a speed of 7,000 miles an hour. These weapons would be used against bunkers and other heavily reinforced ground facilities. Some studies maintain that Rods from God could be fully operational in ten years. Such weapons, which hit the earth with enormous impact, could well be considered weapons of mass destruction, and therefore would violate the 1967 Outer Space Treaty.[37] Again, this system has no advantages over ground-based systems, and is factorially more expensive.

The same cost considerations affect programs using satellites for anti-missile laser weapons, mirrors for reflecting energy beams, and the CAV program. Richard Garwin, considered by many as the dean of American weapons science, wrote in the March 2005 issue of *IEEE Spectrum*, the professional journal of electrical engineering, that "a space-based laser would cost $100 million, compared with $600,000 for a Tomahawk missile."[38]

The United States is not presently developing nuclear weapons in low-earth orbit as a bombardment weapon.[39] However, despite the Outer Space Treaty, future U.S. plans do not rule them out. The Strategic Master Plan FY06 of the Air Force Space Command states, "A viable, prompt global strike capability, whether nuclear or non-nuclear, will allow the US to rapidly and accurately strike distant high-payoff, difficult-to-defeat targets."[40] Rather than entertain such an option, all nations should pledge not to develop, test or deploy nuclear-armed interceptors or weapons and technologies for use in or from outer space. This would, of course, require the immediate retirement of the Russian Galosh nuclear-armed missile defense system over Moscow, which was the missile defense system allowed under the ABM Treaty of 1972 (each side could put up one system).[41]

In November 2003, the "U.S. Air Force Transformation Flight Plan" created a comprehensive listing of weapons under consideration—reconnaissance weapons and intelligence weapons, anti-satellite weapons, and direct-strike weapons. It was clear then, and it is still clearer today, that space dominance is the Bush administration's objective. As the Center for Defense Information writes, "The U.S. military is proceeding apace down a path toward space weaponization in what is essentially a public policy vacuum. There has been little debate among policy-makers and law-makers about the enormous strategic implications of a world with space weapons, and a unilateral U.S. move to become the first to acquire them."[42]

THE ARGUMENTS AGAINST SPACE WEAPONIZATION

The strongest argument against putting American weapons in space is that it will weaken rather than enhance our national security. American weapons in space will incite other countries, such as China and Russia, to take countermeasures, including placing their own weapons in space. This will, of course, justify still further expensive deployments to "protect" U.S. assets from this "new threat." The ensuing arms race in outer space will obviously create still another area in which miscalculations, competition, and aggressive deployment can lead to war. With thousands of nuclear weapons on hair-trigger alert in the United States and Russia, a catastrophic nuclear war could easily ensue.[43]

The weaponization of space could put the United States into direct diplomatic confrontation with the rest of the world. Recent unilateral military actions by the United States have already taken their toll. Authoritative Pew polls show that the United States has slipped badly in its standing with the rest of the world.[44] The United States is now considered by hundreds of millions of people to be the most dangerous country on the planet. This suspicion could descend to genuine hatred if the United States took the position of dominating outer space, and leaving to itself the option of terrorizing the planet by orbiting bombardment satellites.

What an extraordinary change in perception from the years after World War II when the United States was seen by most people in the world as the beacon of hope for world peace and economic prosperity! It championed the United Nations; it supported multilateral control of nuclear weapons, generous foreign aid, and international standards for human rights. Now, the United States has fallen from grace, and the price will be enormous—in international cooperation on vital issues such as terrorism, in countries like Iraq or Afghanistan, and in the handling of international trade and currency issues. The effects are often not immediately apparent—statespeople from other countries do not necessarily issue overt denunciations—but they are real as the United States scrambles for allies in Iraq and other areas of the Middle East, as the dollar falls in relation to other currencies, and as America faces hostile competition in the trading of key commodities.

If the United States weaponizes space, it will pay other huge costs. The move to weaponize outer space will put at risk the entire range of U.S. military and commercial satellites, as well as those involved in scientific exploration. Space expert James Oberg estimates that by 2010, the U.S. investment in space could reach $500 to $600 billion, equaling the value of all current U.S. investments in Europe.[45] Not only would U.S. military satellites be targets, but so would U.S. communication, weather, and observation satellites, particularly because most of these satellites have dual use and are also being used by the military.

Nor can the United States plausibly claim its weapons are defensive. Jamming is offensive, as are kinetic kill vehicles designed to destroy another country's satellites, and, of course, bombardment weapons. All these weapons will be seen as components of a single, aggressive system and foster countermeasures by other space powers, and the ensuing space arms race, as stated above, will increase the likelihood of conflict.

How will other countries react to the U.S. weaponization of outer space, and its attempt to achieve Full Spectrum Dominance? Filmmaker and columnist Michael Moore asks,

> Would you be surprised if Russia or China or any other country announced that it planned to deploy a comprehensive space-control capability? . . . Of course we Americans would be worried, alarmed, angry. What right would any nation have to unilaterally develop the capability to control space and to 'deny' access to others—potentially at a time of its own choosing? If any nation, even a friendly nation, announced such plans, Americans would demand that Washington lean on the offender as hard as needed to force a recantation. Meanwhile, the United States would call upon the international community to impose draconian economic sanctions until that country's policies were reversed.

"But," Moore notes, "if such measures failed, the world would have a new space race. Military dominance of near-space rather than sending men and women to the Moon or possibly Mars would be the goal."[46]

Theresa Hitchens, Director of Space Security at the Center for Defense Information, told a Council on Foreign Relations meeting in 2005 that no nation will "accept the U.S. developing something they see as a death star. I don't think the United States would find it very comforting if China were to develop a death star, a 24/7 on-orbit weapon that could strike targets on the ground anywhere in 90 minutes." And as Nicholas Dunlop, Secretary-General of the e-Parliament, which includes U.S. congressmen and space experts, stated, "It is not unlikely that Chinese military planners, following the discussions of space weapons in the U.S., are making their own worst-case calculations about the consequences for China of U.S. military domination of space. If each side is sufficiently worried about the other, and if each side feels profoundly uninformed about the real activities of the other in space, there is every chance that the worst-case scenarios will become self-fulfilling prophesies."[47] Since the early 1990s, both Russia and China have expressed their apprehensions that if the United States moves to create the capacity to attack their early warning and space surveillance systems and to weaponize space with direct attack weapons, such actions would be seen as a formidable threat to their national security.[48] The Russian space surveillance system, or early warning system, is particularly vulnerable, because it consists of only three satellites which are nearing the end of their operational life. A U.S. attack on this system would pose a distinct danger possibly leading to a nuclear war.

Ambassador Thomas Graham points out:

The United States and Russia maintain thousands of nuclear warheads on long-range ballistic missiles on 15-minute alert. Once launched, they cannot be recalled, and they will strike their targets in roughly 30 minutes. Fifteen years after the end of the Cold War, the chance of an accidental nuclear exchange has far from decreased. . . . Both the United

States and Russia rely on space-based systems to provide early warning of a nuclear attack. If deployed, however, U.S. space-based missile defense interceptors could eliminate the Russian early warning satellites quickly and without warning. . . . The potential protection space-based defenses might offer the United States is swamped therefore by their potential cost: a failure of or false signal from a component of the Russian early warning system could lead to a disastrous reaction and accidental nuclear war. . . . Nor are the Russians or other countries likely to stand still and watch the United States construct space-based defenses. These states are likely to respond by developing advanced anti-satellite weapon systems. These weapons, in turn, would endanger U.S. early warning systems, impair valuable U.S. weapons intelligence efforts, and increase the jitteriness of U.S. officials.[49]

This anticipated reaction thoroughly vitiates the utility of space weaponization in creating national security; far from advancing it, space weapons will put it in serious jeopardy.

Does a policy of Full Spectrum Dominance make any sense? On May 8, 2002, Tom Daschle, Democratic Majority Leader, declared: "I think putting weapons in space may be the single dumbest thing I've heard so far from this administration. It would be a disaster for us to put weapons in space of any kind under any circumstances. I think Democrats will be universally opposed to doing something as foolish as that. It only invites other countries to do the same thing and opens up a whole new array of challenges and threats to national security, the likes of which this administration hasn't even begun to think about."

However, Everett Dolman, Associate Professor of Comparative Military Studies, U.S. Air Force School of Advanced Air and Space Studies, asks, "Can the United States afford to be the second state to weaponize space?" Dolman argues that space is the high ground, which gives the advantage of surveillance and the energy of gravitational force, and could be used to deny any other country the possibility of gaining military access to space.[50] Of course, the Dolman argument implies that if the United States doesn't weaponize outer space, another nation will. But this is highly challengeable. No other nation has the economic and military resources of the United States. Why, in the absence of a clear challenge, would another nation embark on a weaponization policy which would not only be ruinous for its economy, but ultimately unsuccessful, once the United States got into the game? Particularly as China develops its military power over the next decade or two, the policy of Full Spectrum Dominance will look increasingly short-sighted. Presently, because it is so powerful militarily, the United States has a perfect opportunity to remove space from the realm of warfare. If it does not, it will inevitably face the consequences of having failed to act.

Nevertheless, the United States gives every appearance of going ahead with plans for outer space dominance. In his May 2005 *New York Times* article, Tim Weiner reported that the "Air Force, saying it must secure space to protect the nation from attack, is seeking President Bush's approval of a national-security directive that could move the United States closer to fielding offensive and defensive space weapons, according to White House and Air Force officials."[51] As the world's dominant power, the United States hardly needs to open still another theater of dominance, particularly when other nations are quite willing to keep space outside the area of military competition. This being so, and if the United States can secure peaceful space assets without resort to weapons, how and why is it now moving steadily toward weaponization? What possible gain can be achieved, either for U.S. security or for its peaceful and commercial interest, except to extend the hegemonic dreams of those presently in power and to provide funds for industries, such as Boeing and Lockheed Martin?

The costs of such weaponization will indeed be formidable. The Bush administration has already awarded huge contracts to the major corporations in the field.[52] It is difficult to know exactly how far research and development of space weaponization have progressed, and how much money has been spent. Theresa Hitchens points out that "one-half of DOD spending on space is classified. We do know that total DOD spending in space—both classified and unclassified—is about $22.5 billion in FY '06, and this figure is expected to increase by at least $1 billion a year over the next six years."[53] The difficulties of analyzing the space budget—because many items are classified, are included under other heads, or blacked out for security reasons, and component parts are separated—create a budgetary nightmare for analysts.[54] Suffice it to say that a figure of $22.5 billion is huge and threatening. But the space race itself, once started, could end up costing the United States hundreds of billions, if not trillions of dollars.

THE PROBLEMS OF SPACE DEBRIS, RADIO FREQUENCIES, AND ORBITAL SLOTS

The testing of missile defense systems is *already* posing a danger to people and spacecraft by its production of debris. Due to the very high speeds in low orbit—about 10 kilometers per second—particles less than one-tenth of a millimeter in diameter can damage a spacecraft. Debris only ten centimeters in diameter in low-earth orbit have the same destructive power as a 35,000 kilogram truck moving at 190 kilometers an hour, sufficient to lead to the loss of a spacecraft. When debris in low-earth orbit returns to earth intact, it poses a lethal danger to people and to property.

Presently, there are about 13,000 objects large enough—10 centimeters in diameter—to seriously damage or destroy a spacecraft in orbit. Over 90 percent of these objects are debris. In addition, scientists estimate that there are tens of millions of objects between 1 and 10 centimeters, which can also cause satellite damage. Satellite shielding can protect satellites from these small pieces of debris; only maneuvering of a threatened satellite can protect it from the larger pieces, and maneuvering is quite expensive due to the cost of sending the necessary fuel into orbit. In geostationary orbit, debris speeds are somewhat slower, about the speed of a rifle bullet, but debris is still highly destructive. Pieces of debris in geosynchronous orbit, because they will not return to earth as they eventually will in low-earth orbit, remain a threat for centuries.

Clearly, mid-course missile defense, which shatters missiles in outer space, poses enormous dangers because it will create massive amounts of debris. The same kinds of dangers would be created by space-based interceptors.[55] If there were hundreds of interceptors in low-earth orbit, as presently projected in one system being researched, the dangers would be immense, because the interceptors themselves could collide with already existing debris, as well as producing debris themselves, creating space-based turmoil.

On September 1, 2004, the Pentagon's Missile Defense Agency released its "Draft Programmatic Environmental Impact Statement on the testing and employment of its future ballistic missile defense system." According to Theresa Hitchens, the report radically underestimates the amount of debris produced and also inaccurately states that most of it will return to earth in a short period of time.[56]

While many countries, including China, the EU, Japan, Russia, and the United States, have developed standards for minimizing debris in space, and the issue is being dealt with in the United Nations, debris caused by military activity remains beyond the reach of regulation, and poses a huge danger to the peaceful uses of outer space.

Today, the rate of creation of new debris in space is actually slackening, due in part to a number of international agreements that regulate how much debris can be released in launch and in flight, and to efforts by space powers to mitigate debris caused by their launches. Such agreements also call for dead satellites in lower orbits to be removed within twenty-five years, and for satellites in geosynchronous orbit to be kicked up some 235 kilometers higher into graveyard orbits, leaving the lower orbits for communication and other satellites, although such actions significantly increase the costs of using the satellites. The amount of debris will be radically increased, however, if the United States and other space powers test and deploy more complex missile defense systems and weaponize outer space.

As Hitchens points out, harm to the space environment is prohibited by the 1967 Outer Space Treaty, as well as other conventions. The reason this provision of the treaty must be honored today is that satellites in outer space have created a world communication system, global information exchange, a global positioning system, outer space exploration, outer space monitored arms control, and other services that are a vital part of our modern world.

Another of the casualties to be incurred by the weaponization of space, in addition to the destruction wrought by debris, is the co-opting of scarce radio frequencies and orbital slots. As the peaceful scientific and commercial operations in space increase yearly, so does their reliance on radio frequencies and their need for orbital paths, particularly in geosynchronous orbit. These issues are handled by the International Telecommunications Union, although the ITU has no means of actually enforcing its agreements, and members may avoid following ITU rules by invoking national defense requirements. A major problem is that a country that deploys a military satellite is reluctant to disclose its orbital slot and radio frequency, fearing that such information could be used by an adversary to track the satellite, with the possibility of shooting it down, or jamming its signal. Another is that countries, particularly the United States, put in requests to reserve orbital slots they may not use for several years, thus monopolizing the diminishing number of orbital slots, particularly in geosynchronous orbit. These actions have rightly become a source of international tension.[57] As reported by Theresa Hitchens, "According to Adm. James Ellis, commander of U.S. Strategic Command, the U.S. military demand for bandwidth is practically endless. 'We've got no clear view of when it might slow down,' he said. 'I believe that it will almost certainly never stop—the only question is the pace at which it continues to grow.' "[58]

These problems will move from difficult to chronic as nations, particularly the United States, start launching their weapons into outer space. The U.S. attitude to these scarce resources reminds us of its blithe disregard for scarce energy resources, such as oil, where it has taken no action in decades to reduce its use, and today consumes 25 percent of the world's energy with only 5 percent of the world's population. When it comes to the delicate issue of orbital slots and radio frequencies, the world simply cannot afford to allow the United States to commandeer these scarce resources.

The solution to the problem of space debris and the scarcity of radio frequencies and orbital slots is rigorous international regulation, using international organizations like the Committee on the Peaceful Uses of Outer Space of the United Nations and the International Telecommunications Union, as well as creative legislation to be enacted by the space powers themselves (see Chapter 5). The more space is militarized, and in particular, the more it is weaponized, the less likely it is that any adequate set of regulations will eventuate.

Military Satellites

Problems are created by the sheer numbers of military satellites. By the end of 2003, the United States and Russia had launched more than 2,000 military satellites, while the rest of the world had launched fewer than 40.[59] The major player, however, is the United States, which today accounts for 95 percent of the world's military space expenditures and maintains 135 operational military satellites—over half of all military satellites in orbit.[60] Russia is the number-two space military power, although between 70 and 80 percent of its satellites have passed their effective life span. China has a few satellites to maintain navigational capacity in case the United States cuts off its GPS services in time of conflict, and a couple more for tactical reconnaissance and surveillance, although at the moment it is attempting to rapidly expand that number. The European Union is also moving into military satellites, as is Israel, India, and Japan.[61]

These developments make clear, however, that if the United States were to move into space weaponization, such a move would be vigorously opposed by other threatened states. While relations between the United States, Russia, and the European Union are not very tense currently, the human history of militarism and nationalism gives one little security that such relationships could not degenerate into outright hostility should the United States embark on a provocative course of space weaponization.

According to Dr. Rebecca Johnson, Executive Director of the Acronym Institute for Disarmament Diplomacy in London, Europe is eager not to offend the U.S. government, and is trying to avoid a confrontation on this issue. However, she declares, "Europeans cannot sit back and wait for all the decisions to be taken before they react to protect their interests in space."[62]

The Europeans are beginning now to ask themselves if they can afford to be concerned only with the commercial aspects of space. In a publication of the Centre for European Reform, Daniel Keohane, research fellow for security and defense policy, asks, "should the EU aspire to merely an economic power, or should it aim for a more credible common foreign and security policy? . . . And more specifically, is the EU's stated ambition of being able to manage autonomous military operations realistic, unless it develops satellite networks that can operate independently of America's space assets?" Jacques Chirac, President of France, has argued that unless Europe develops its own satellite capabilities, it will remain little more than a "vassal" of the United States.[63] Relations with Russia could degenerate easily, and Chinese–American relations are already tense, and could get worse. Behind these concerns are the development of independent global positioning systems, such as the EU's Galileo, as well as communication and observation satellites that have dual military and peaceful purposes. Space rivalry, which today is confined to these types of satellites, would explode into an arms race should the United States up the ante by weaponizing outer space. In early March 2006, Russia's ambassador to the UN office in Geneva, Vallery Loshchinin, said that the placement of weapons in space would "provoke a new round of the race for nuclear missiles and other arms . . . which would boost the proliferation of weapons of mass destruction and their delivery vehicles."[64]

· War in outer space would so poison relations between countries that the intense cooperation many outer space projects require, both commercial and scientific, would be sharply curtailed. In its plans to weaponize outer space, the United States seems prepared to sacrifice precious peaceful uses for dubious military advantage. Even if the United States did succeed in militarizing space, it would have achieved a nerve-wracking state; space would be unstable, punctuated by challenges to U.S. dominance and a worldwide state of tension, perhaps worse than the Cold War.

The implications of weaponization—enormous costs, risking the entire range of peaceful services arrayed in outer space, and most importantly, the decrease in U.S. security associated with these provocative moves, and the possibility of a space war—compel the United States to explore alternatives. The world is now ready to accept a diplomatic solution to the horrendous problems posed by the weaponization of outer space. It is ready to sign rigorous international agreements that would permanently bar weapons from space, and create the sanctuary of outer space for peaceful purposes.

The United States must immediately move away from its bellicose stance, and embrace diplomacy. Now, when it has military superiority, is the time to work out the agreements that will ensure its future.

5

Alternatives to Weapons in Outer Space

The stars at night
Are big and bright
Deep in the heart of Texas
　　　　—From the song, "Deep in the Heart of Texas"[1]

In the next two decades, new technologies will allow
the field of space-based weapons of devastating effec-
tiveness to be used to deliver energy and mass as force
projection in tactical and strategic conflict. These ad-
vances will enable lasers with reasonable mass and cost
to effect many kills. This can be done rapidly, continu-
ously and with surgical precision, minimizing exposure
of friendly forces. The technologies exist or can be de-
veloped in this time period.
　　　　—U.S. Air Force Advisory Board, 1996[2]

Now is the time to stop weapons in space. Not ten years from now, or even five or two, when more major contracts have been awarded, but now before the momentum builds and there is no turning back. Most of us are currently unaware that the weaponization of space is occurring and cannot imagine the ways in which it will irrevocably alter the future of life on the planet.

Today more than at any other time in the nation's history, control over the military, and the direction of military policy, has slipped out of the hands of the people and their representatives in Congress, and into the hands of a tight little cabal in the Executive Branch. Information about the development of military programs, including outer space, is not shared with those in Congress responsible under the Constitution for policy and appropriations; and the president has allocated unto himself sweeping powers under a continuous, undefined war on terror, and the privilege of interpreting laws according to his own private views. With the shift to Democratic control of Congress on November 7, 2006, it is likely, however, that this blackout of information will end.

The results of these policies have been seen in the catastrophic situation in Iraq, in the unchecked growth of the "black box" defense budget, in executive decisions to defy treaties such as the Nuclear Non-Proliferation and Outer Space Treaties, and in threats issued to other countries of pre-emptive war in violation of the UN Charter. In enacting these policies, the president and his inner circle have turned their backs on long-standing U.S. policies that emerged at the end of World War II. At that time in history, the United States took the lead in stressing multilateral obligations under the UN and other treaties, in using its resources for foreign economic aid rather than armaments, and in attempting to establish a world ruled not by force but by international law.[3] To be sure, during the Cold War the country was constrained to defend itself against the Soviet threat. But today, an unchallenged United States is employing unprecedented unilateral force. In no area is this stance clearer than in the American drive to weaponize space.

In this book we must examine alternatives to space weaponization. Then the citizenry must be mobilized and the Congress must be inspired to act in the interests of the people of the United States and the world, rather than the interests of weapons manufacturers and power-hungry operatives in the U.S. government.

If the United States weaponizes outer space, energy needs will expand to fuel launches and space weapons, and also to fuel the expanding military-space economy as nations begin to compete with the United States in outer space. As pointed out by two of the most profound analysts of the energy problem, Michael T. Klare, author of *Blood and Oil,* and Edward O. Wilson, author of

The Future of Life, petroleum resources will become increasingly scarce with rising population and income levels around the world, and will inevitably bring major national consumers into conflict. The European Union, for instance, whose economy and population exceed those of the United States, spends about a quarter as much of its income on arms as America does. But this is a reversible situation, if the EU is faced with a major shortage of oil which could cripple its economy. One of the reasons that the EU is developing the Galileo alternative satellite positioning system is undoubtedly because of future competition over scarce resources, such as oil.

China, with a GNP growth rate of 8 percent, a population of 1.3 billion people and increasing energy needs, is already in political conflict with the United States in Sudan and Iran, as is the Russian Federation. Such conflicts will inevitably be exacerbated as these countries' oil needs grow. New discoveries of oil will prove to be inadequate, as the world's oil supply is projected to flatten and even diminish. Oil-rich areas within the old Soviet empire, the South China Sea, the Caspian Sea, and areas of Africa such as Nigeria, not to mention the Middle East, will increasingly become areas of conflict. Many of these areas are already hosting foreign military missions, receiving armaments, and being co-opted to favor the United States, Russia, or China.[4] As global oil supplies diminish, the need to secure oil resources will become increasingly acute, creating inevitable conflicts. As the United States devotes more and more of its resources to military endeavors, including those in outer space, it will project itself into conflicts over the resources that it needs to maintain dominance.

Arming for a war in outer space will consume hundreds of billions, if not trillions of dollars of scarce resources, and will result in the cutting off of aid to the developing world, permanently depressing standards of living. As the world confronts global poverty and sets its Millennium Goals, as we see tens of millions of children dying needlessly every year, whole countries decimated by curable diseases, and millions of lives lost in endless cycles of poverty, it is an act of moral degradation to spend vital funds on a project so useless and wickedly destructive as weaponizing outer space.

In the war on terrorism, for example, would the United States better spend its resources on economic aid than on space weaponization? Economist Jeffrey D. Sachs points out:

> Almost three thousand people died needlessly and tragically at the World Trade Center on September 11; ten thousand Africans die needlessly and tragically every single day—and have died every single day since September 11—of AIDS, TB, and malaria. . . . To fight terrorism, we will need to fight poverty and deprivation as well. A purely military approach to terrorism is doomed to fail. Just as a doctor fights disease by prescribing not only medication, but also by bolstering a person's immune system through adequate nutrition and by encouraging a healthy lifestyle for his patients, so, too, we need to address the underlying weaknesses of the societies in which terrorism lurks—extreme poverty; mass unmet needs for jobs, incomes and dignity; and the political and economic instability that results from degrading human conditions.[5]

Rather than meet the modest Millennium Goals of giving .7 percent of its income for economic aid, the United States has delivered only .17 percent. (During the Marshall Plan after World War II, the United States contributed over 2 percent of its income, and reaped the benefits of a strong, democratic Europe.) Here again, the Bush administration, obsessed with military adventures, like the weaponization of space, is jeopardizing the long-term stability of the country.

The same issue can be seen domestically. With a budget strained by military expenses, the reaction of the Bush administration to

Hurricanes Katrina and Rita was to cut domestic programs for the poor, rather than stop or reduce tax cuts for the wealthy. These policies have continued with more cuts to the poor and increasing tax breaks for the rich. Neither has the Bush administration contemplated reducing grossly unnecessary military spending, partially created by a useless missile defense system, and by an impending arms race in outer space. Quite the contrary: military budgets go up annually, with expenditures on outer space rising a billion dollars a year. How can the Bush administration in conscience cut benefits to the needy when it has the option of cutting needless expenditures on armaments? And can the United States afford to increase its national debt to the point that it jeopardizes its total financial stability? The United States is currently faced with a far more promising option—diplomacy.

Faced with an arms race in outer space, with vast assets devoted to the peaceful uses of outer space in jeopardy, with impending conflicts over energy, and with the unmet needs of the poor here and abroad, the United States must begin work on diplomatic solutions rather than resorting to unilateral assertions of force. There is some nascent hope that such an option could be exercised. Diplomacy has not been the option of first choice for the Bush administration during its first term, but it is gaining some recent traction. For four years, Colin Powell, Secretary of State, was not included in the Bush inner circle, and clearly did not carry much weight with the cabal of militarists headed by Vice President Cheney and Secretary of Defense Rumsfeld. Now that Condoleezza Rice, a long-time advisor and confidant of the president, is Secretary of State, diplomatic options are becoming somewhat more possible although to date, Rice generally has not used her influence in the Bush inner group to promote diplomacy. The Bush administration has not fared well in its reliance on force and threats of force in Iraq, North Korea, and Iran. The United States also faces mounting budgetary deficits that threaten the stability of the economy, and the possibility of a financial crash that would handicap and mar the Republican Party for years.

Diplomacy often progresses not by initial major treaties, but by small, incremental steps that build confidence and create the atmosphere in which larger solutions are possible. These steps, which may or may not be defined by legal agreements, create a body of practice that leads to larger solutions. If war is the ultimate breakdown of confidence, peace is the result of small measures that create and reinforce confidence.

A major initial ingredient of such confidence, which needs to be practiced by the current space powers, is greater transparency. Bilateral or multilateral transparency on space budgets, candid discussions among military and civilian government experts about their current and intended space programs, agreements on cooperative international measures for space surveillance in order to track any unusual activity by satellites, and negotiations for international inspection of space launches must be instituted immediately.

Transparency and openness will be essential for tracking space debris, for verifying compliance with orbital slot allocations, and for avoiding collisions in space. Transparency is also a vital first step for any diplomatic solution leading to the establishment of international agreements on the de-weaponization of outer space. Transparency limits fear among competitors about each others' intentions, and decreases the risk of a space arms race.

As Nicholas Dunlop, Secretary-General of the e-Parliament, reports, "Transparency is a subject of interest to everyone. Whatever their position on the deployment of space weapons, all sides showed interest in having rules of the road . . . to avoid unintentional conflicts in space. For example, prior warning of the movements of satellites is one aspect of transparency. There is understood to be significant interest in the U.S. Defense Department in exploring cooperating with the Europeans and others on a comprehensive system of space surveillance."[6] Such a system would lessen tension around space launches. Transparency with the Chinese, for example, would be particularly useful in reassuring members of Congress about Chinese intentions in outer space.

RULES OF THE ROAD FOR INTERNATIONAL CONDUCT IN OUTER SPACE

"Rules of the road" are established international procedures that regulate practices that benefit the nations concerned, and give them confidence in the peaceful intent of their global neighbors. Such rules can provide the level of confidence needed to move toward more formal international agreements. In the field of outer space, a number of areas offer a clear opening for such rules of the road.

Debris

The first area is the problem of space debris. Last year, debris grew by 2.1 percent.[7] While this growth was not dramatic, debris could totally disrupt the peaceful uses of outer space should space be weaponized. A present set of rules are at hand to keep debris at workable levels. Theresa Hitchens of the Center for Defense Information suggests that the UN Committee on the Peaceful Uses of Outer Space should adopt the debris mitigation guidelines developed by the Inter-Agency Space Debris Coordination Committee, and solidify these resolutions with a UN resolution. U.S. legislation should make sure that these guidelines become national policy, and the technical details negotiated to ensure that they become the international standard, and are then adopted. Finally, the Liability Convention should be amended to create penalties for space operators who fail to comply with internationally agreed guidelines.

Radio Spectrum and Orbital Slots

An international solution also exists for the problems of allocating the radio spectrum for communication with satellites and for assigning them orbital slots. The International Telecommunications Union and satellite users need to negotiate and agree on better methods to decrease radio frequency interference and share the radio spectrum. Countries that book orbits and frequencies to hold in reserve (the United States and France are today the worst offenders) should be prevented from doing this by the imposition of fines and by strict regulations.

At present the ITU has no enforcement powers for frequency allocation or orbital slots, and compliance is usually avoided by nations citing national defense requirements. Also, users of orbital slots do not currently need to report when their satellite has maneuvered out of its allocated slot. These problems with orbital slots are particularly serious for the geostationary slots, and need to be corrected, as they can be through international agreements.[8]

Ballistic Missile Proliferation

In the last fifteen years, more than a dozen countries have renounced or limited their missile programs, and very few countries are actually building ballistic missiles. More than thirty countries have agreed not to transfer missiles and missile technology to other countries, and more than hundred have signed the Hague Code of Conduct against Ballistic Missile Proliferation. This movement has recently been put in some jeopardy by a new U.S. plan to put conventional bombs on ICBMs, a shift in policy advocated by former U.S. Secretaries of Defense Harold Brown and Arthur Schlesinger. By lifting the sanction against using ICBMs, some experts fear the United States will make it more attractive for countries to develop their own ICBMs.[9] The United States should reconsider this policy, as it jeopardizes an international movement that is making the world safer.

Satellite Registration

All satellites should be registered and their purpose identified, a move which could form the basis of other international agreements limiting or eliminating the weaponization of outer space. Although the United States and other space powers have failed to register most of their current military satellites, this policy would need to be immediately reversed, so that all satellites were clearly registered, a movement which in itself would boost security and confidence.

Lowering Tension

Even before a necessary agreement on the banning of space weapons is signed, methods are available for lowering tensions. States should attempt to define dangerous military activities and seek methods for avoiding them. International agreements are often most effective when they codify already existing practice. A good start toward "rules of the road," or agreed-upon practices, was articulated by The Henry L. Stimson Center in a "Model Code of Conduct for the Prevention of Incidents and Dangerous Military Practices in Outer Space."

The Code lists dangerous military practices that must be avoided, including:

- Simulating an attack on a satellite;
- Increasing the risk of collision or failing to reduce the risk of collision in space;
- Using a directed energy device, including a laser, to disrupt, degrade, impair, or destroy a satellite; and
- Flight testing or deploying an anti-satellite or a space weapon.

To implement these provisions, the Code calls on states to:

- Give prior notice of a peaceful approach to another satellite;
- Provide special caution zones around satellites;
- Avoid actions which can be seen as threatening;
- Provide adequate launch information and registration of satellites;
- Follow internationally set standards for mitigating debris;
- Follow International Telecommunications Union recommendations on spectrum use and orbital slot allocation;
- Use verification methods in accordance with international law; and
- Set up and use a communication and consultation system to avoid misunderstandings.[10]

These provisions should be part of any binding treaty designed to ensure the peaceful uses of outer space.[11] But short of such a treaty, the institution of these practices would be a major step toward deweaponization. The codifying of such practices in strict international agreements would be a "next step," after such confidence-building measures have already been carried out in practice.

Monitoring rules of the road, of course, remains a problem. As Michael Krepon points out, "While the monitoring of rules of the road need not be as stringent as for treaty obligations, it still must be sufficient to provide assurance of compliance and early warning of misbehavior." He warns, "Some monitoring tasks for rules of the road may, indeed, prove to be extremely difficult to operationalize."[12] Nevertheless, such monitoring needs to be undertaken. Precisely because of the difficulties, as soon as such monitoring is instituted, a process is established that clears away difficulties and prepares for the more formal monitoring procedures of an international agreement.

DIPLOMATIC SOLUTIONS

The next step, after stating principles and asking for voluntary compliance, is the creation of rigorous treaties. Such treaties can happen only if the United States and other powers restrain their testing and deployment of anti-satellite and bombardment weapons, as deployment will be both threatening and difficult to reverse. Also required is a willingness, particularly by the United States, to accede to international agreements that will almost certainly be seen as limiting U.S. sovereignty or its capacity for unilateral action. The United States's refusal to sign on to the Comprehensive Nuclear Test Ban, the International Criminal Court, the Kyoto Protocols, and other agreements attests to the lack of willingness by the Bush administration to conform to international norms. Just as the United States, which once opposed the League of Nations, was able to achieve the vision of international cooperation with the United Nations, so here, too, the United States must overcome its preoccupation with unilateral hegemony, and work with other nations in achieving an international regime for the regulation and peaceful uses of outer space. In so doing, the United States will have the support of the rest of the world, including the other major space powers.[13]

Canadian, Russian, and Chinese Willingness to Move Toward a Treaty on De-Weaponization

At the "Full Spectrum Dominance" Conference, May 16–17, 2005, delegates from Canada, Russia, and China gave clear indications of their governments' interest in securing a binding treaty. In so doing, they questioned the U.S. contention that its moves to weaponize outer space would be defensive. In proposing a binding international treaty, these nations challenged the United States to rise to the higher ground of international cooperation.

Dr. John Polanyi, Professor of Chemistry at the University of Toronto, co-editor of *The Dangers of Nuclear War*, and winner of the Nobel Prize (1986), stated that despite their enormous differences on other issues, Canada's "four political parties form part of a Canadian national consensus that the weaponization of space would be deplorable." One reason for this, he said, is that the Canadian public is better informed on outer space issues and has reached its own conclusions, which is not evident in the United States. This feeling has led Canada to reject the U.S. invitation to participate in continental missile defense.

According to Dr. Polanyi, Canada is committed to international law, whose pioneers, he pointed out, can be found in the United States, which was central to establishing the League of Nations, the Nuremburg Trials, the Atlantic Charter, the United Nations, the Universal Declaration of Human Rights, the Genocide Convention, and the International Monetary Fund, among others. Dr. Polanyi made clear that the scientific and technological revolutions that have transformed the world require a transformation of human behavior. Technology moves too fast to allow technological proficiency to permit a single country to stay ahead. This means that national security can best be achieved not by a frantic race to maintain technical superiority in outer space but by the prevention of weaponization through agreement under international law.

By contrast, Polanyi cited the reports of the Rumsfeld panels, which argued that space war was a virtual certainty. The solution offered was not restraint but single-nation dominance. Yet the United States, Polanyi maintained, is the nation that has argued persistently that security is a collective responsibility. In calling for democracy everywhere, President Bush himself has asserted that human choices move events, and that such choices should be democratic, or shared. The Space Treaty of 1967, which the United States championed, has been reenforced by repeated resolutions of the UN General Assembly. Today, the United States has the opportunity, Polanyi asserted, to preclude weaponization through democratically chosen international law. "The establishment of law is . . . a task that offers hope. The same cannot be claimed for a return to the jungle." The opportunity to establish such law must be seized now—"the opportunity will not come again."[14]

Similar views were expressed by Dr. Vladimir Yermakov, Senior Counselor at the Russian Embassy in Washington. Russia, Yermakov pointed out, was the first nation, in 1957, to put its assets in outer space, and for this reason has a clear idea of the dangers of the irresponsible use of outer space. International law, however, does not currently prohibit the placing in space of weapons that are not weapons of mass destruction. In addition, when the United States withdrew from the Anti-Ballistic Missile (ABM Treaty) in December of 2001, it opened the door for the development of space-based missile defense systems, which had been prohibited by the treaty.

These disturbing possibilities, Dr. Yermakov made clear in 2005, have prompted Russia to call for an international treaty on the de-weaponization of outer space. Dr. Yermakov stated,

> The progress of science and technology, especially the research and development of weapons to be used in space warfare, as well as the development of military doctrines which include the concept of weaponization of outer space, make it necessary for the international community to think thoroughly about a new global strategy of space security. There is an urgent need for a solid and reliable international legal structure which could provide for further common outer space activities to become not a danger for mankind but an advanced instrument of a comprehensive progressive development of every nation in the world. The issue of preventing the deployment of weapons in outer space and thus preventing an arms race in outer space is one of our strategic stability priorities.

Weaponization of space by one country, Yermakov made clear, would be met by countermeasures by others, and would inevitably destroy the entire fabric of arms control agreements. It would also disrupt the peaceful uses of outer space which are so important to the world, particularly by its creation of destructive space debris.

Specifically, Yermakov proposed resumption of the work of the Conference on Disarmament's Ad Hoc Committee on an International Treaty on the De-Weaponization of Outer Space, the Threat or Use of Force against Outer Space Objects, as proposed by Russia and China. "This treaty should lay down three basic obligations: not to place in orbit around the earth any objects carrying any kind of weapons, not to install such weapons on celestial bodies, and not to station such weapons in outer space in any other manner."

At the 56th Session of the General Assembly, Russia had proposed a moratorium on placing combat devices in outer space, pending an agreement on this issue by the international community. In October 2002, Russia declared that it would accept greater transparency, and has implemented this by having all information on its scheduled outer space launches available at a Web site. Last October, it declared that Russia would not be the first nation to place weapons of any kind in outer space. "Now," Yermakov declared in 2005, "we call upon all nations of the world to follow our example." Such a step could "promote an environment of mutual trust and create favorable political and psychological conditions" to start the elaboration of a binding treaty.

At the Full Spectrum Dominance Conference, Ambassador Jonathan Dean, political advisor for the Union of Concerned Scientists and former U.S. Representative to the NATO-Warsaw Pact force reduction negotiations in Vienna, pointed out, "If several spacefaring countries joined in a declaration like this, this action would form a rudimentary space weapons treaty." Such a commitment would be valid only so long as nations adhered to it, and it could include an agreement to cooperate with other governments to develop effective methods of verification. Such a resolution, he said, could also be used to popularize a possible treaty against weapons in space.

Action limiting outer space weaponization could take place in the context of Vladimir Putin's current support for nuclear disarmament. On June 27, 2006, he urged the United States to open talks on a weapons treaty to replace the key START agreement. "We call for the renewal of dialogue on key weapons reduction issues—first of all, we propose to our American partners to launch negotiations on replace the START treaty," Putin said, adding that it was necessary to help reverse what he called a period of "stagnation" in disarmament.[15]

Dr. Hui Zhang, Research Associate at Harvard University's John F. Kennedy School of Government, confirmed at the conference that the future of outer space is a topic of national discussion in China, which is concerned that space security be maintained including freedom from attacks of its satellites.[16] He stated that the Chinese "think the real purpose for U.S. space weapons and space control is for space domination. Right now there are no threats to U.S. space assets from other countries. [Space domination] would offer the U.S. absolute military and strategic superiority. And this could be used to interfere with Chinese affairs, such as the Taiwan issue. . . . The second point for Chinese concern is that space weaponization would lead to an arms race in outer space and run this risk of turning outer space into a battlefield." Hegemony, unilateralism, and exceptionalism are too often the themes of American foreign policy, Dr. Zhang declared.

Dr. Zhang explained that the biggest present threat is the American ground-based anti-missile system, which Americans think could neutralize Chinese ICBMs. A first strike on Chinese facilities could reduce their numbers to a very few missiles, which could then have a limited chance of penetrating a missile defense system. China is thinking of converting its fixed silo-based system into a mobile system, but, Dr. Zhang maintained, the United States is already talking of creating the capacity to destroy this system as well. Aggressive U.S. statements about China and U.S. talk of cooperation with Taiwan on tactical missile defense have heightened this concern. According to Dr. Zhang, China has a rich program of commercial satellites, has launched twenty-seven foreign-made satellites for other countries, and has conducted manned space flight. It is understandably concerned that these assets be protected. It is particularly concerned about space debris, which is the necessary consequence of any conflict in space resulting from space weaponization.

Rather than move in this direction, Dr. Zhang urged the United States to think of legal or diplomatic solutions. This would mean a ban of weapons in space and the banning of the use or threat of force against space targets from earth-based weapons. Arms control measures could permit no testing or use of any kind of anti-satellite weapons. Such an agreement would also prohibit space-based missiles. The United States could not insist on having space-based missiles if anti-satellite weapons were prohibited.

If the United States does not proceed with missile defense, estimates are that by 2015, China would have less than fifty warheads deployed against the United States; but if the United States does proceed with missile defense, China would build 100–300, with technically more sophisticated nuclear warheads.[17] China would also develop anti-satellites, and it would also reconsider its participation in the Fissile Material Cutoff Treaty, which would ban the production of fissile material for nuclear weapons or nuclear explosive devices. China would also reconsider its ratification of the Comprehensive Nuclear Test Ban. The direction in which China decides to go on these important issues, Dr. Zhang declared, lies with the United States. The position outlined by Dr. Zhang has been officially confirmed by China in its support of an annual resolution at the UN General Assembly for nations to refrain from actions contrary to the peaceful uses of outer space, and to negotiate an international agreement on the prevention of an outer space arms race.

It is clear from these impressive testimonies that the choice to move toward space weaponization is virtually entirely in U.S. hands. Russia and China—the two countries that could possibly threaten the United States—are committed to an international treaty banning space weaponization, and are willing to talk. It is up to the United States sharply to alter its course and join the world community in a comprehensive treaty.

SHAPING INTERNATIONAL AGREEMENTS TO DE-WEAPONIZE OUTER SPACE

Given the position of Canada, Russia, and China, the United States must begin the process of moving toward a viable treaty on the de-weaponization of outer space. A body of diplomatic agreements already exists that forms the basis of such an advance, the Outer Space Treaty of 1967, the Registration Convention of 1975, the Liability Convention in 1979, and the Moon Treaty in the same year. The Registration Agreement, in particular, could be tightened,[18] and the Moon Treaty signed.

The Moon Treaty has not been signed by the major space powers because states object to its provisions restricting the exploitation of the Moon's natural resources, and the right it grants to states to inspect all space vehicles, equipment, facilities, and installations belonging to any other party. Here again, this agreement could be reappraised and either signed in its original form by the major space powers, or altered in such a way that it would clearly designate the Moon and other celestial bodies as space sanctuaries.

A host of other agreements are moving in the right direction. One example is the 1989 Prevention of Dangerous Military Activities Agreement (PDMA), which establishes procedures for countries not to interfere with or damage the military forces, command centers, and equipment of other countries during peacetime, procedures that could limit dangerous outer space military activities.[19]

Agreements including the Nuclear Non-Proliferation Treaty, the START I and START II treaties, indeed most treaties concerning nuclear weapons, could be transformed into agreements relating to outer space, as nuclear and outer space warfare have always been linked together. However, the Bush administration and other nuclear powers have undercut the Nuclear Non-Proliferation Treaty by refusing to come through on a major provision—divestment by the nuclear powers of their nuclear arms under Article VI. At the five-year United Nations review conference of the NPT in May 2005, the United States scuttled any progress, and kept up its obstructive tactics at the Summit Conference in the fall. This has led to a concerted effort by twenty-eight non-nuclear states, called the Middle Powers Initiative, to put pressure on the United States and other nuclear powers to fulfill their obligations under the Nuclear Non-Proliferation Treaty.

Penalties for Failure to Act

Treaties already exist today that could be used to prevent or inhibit weaponization of space. At the "Full Spectrum Dominance" Conference in May 2005, Ambassador Jonathan Dean made clear that if the United States "perseveres in moving toward weaponization of space, the legal regime could be used to block or delay these moves." At present, he pointed out, the 1967 Outer Space Treaty permits the transit of outer space by nuclear missiles, and the orbiting of non-nuclear weapons to attack other satellites or bombard the earth. However, the Liability Convention of 1972 establishes procedures for determining the liability of a country that damages or destroys the space objects of another country, and the Registration Convention of 1976 requires the registration of objects launched into space. In addition, the Outer Space Treaty itself makes signatories to the treaty who launch objects into space liable for the damage they do to the space assets of another power. It also provides for consultations with other governments if a party to the treaty believes that an activity planned by another treaty party could cause potentially harmful interference with activities in the peaceful exploration and use of outer space.

Consultations under these treaty provisions would constitute an early warning that complications could follow practices that violate these provisions. Beyond this, Ambassador Dean maintained, the UN General Assembly, disposed to limit the military uses of space, could ask for an advisory opinion from the International Criminal Court in The Hague to determine whether the United States moves toward weaponization are in compliance with the Outer Space Treaty. If the United States refused to comply, nations could request an injunction from the Court.

Another agency that might be used, according to Ambassador Dean, is the International Telecommunications Union. A statute of the ITU prohibits harmful interference with satellite communication. This provision could be invoked in the event of frequent jamming or weapons deployment by the United States or other nations.

Still another method that could be used to inhibit belligerent moves into space are declarations from the First Committee of the UN General Assembly. If the United States wished to create a peaceful venue in outer space, it could take the lead in having the committee pass a resolution prohibiting interference with all unarmed satellites. Noncompliance could carry the provisions of direct referral to the Security Council. Dean stated his belief that the United States has "such dominance in the space field that it can afford to try measures like this and then still be far ahead if it decides the measure is not working."

Dean pointed out, "If the United States does not move on this issue, many people are considering going to the General Assembly for a mandate to begin negotiations outside the Conference on Disarmament on a treaty to ban all weapons in outer space." Even if the United States didn't want to move this quickly, preliminary discussions could be held, and Russia, China, and other interested parties could draw up the provisions of a draft treaty.

International agreement rather than space dominance is, Dean believes, in the ultimate interest of the United States.

> There are no commanding heights in space which, once seized, can assure enduring advantage or dominance or which might prevent an arms race in space. None. The United States is not safer today for having initiated the development of the ultimate weapon sixty years ago and for having sought to maintain sole possession of these weapons. To the contrary, the American government and the American people worry day and night that these weapons may come back at them and at others. This same fate will in time attend the possible weaponization of space. That is why it is a vital interest of all governments and all peoples to prevent that weaponization.

ACTION IN THE UNITED NATIONS

In moving toward an effective treaty, the most important diplomatic task is to deal with the present deficiencies of the 1967 Outer Space Treaty: it has no verification or enforcement procedures; it does not forbid conventional weapons in outer space, only weapons of mass destruction; and it does not prohibit anti-satellite weapons based on the ground. Again, these deficiencies could be corrected in a new diplomatic move to de-weaponize outer space. The fact that the 1967 Treaty has been honored for almost forty years creates a useful precedent for its possible extension.

One way to prohibit weaponization of space would be to add a protocol to the Outer Space Treaty stating that the prohibition of nuclear weapons in Article IV of the Treaty shall be extended to weapons of any kind, whether in space, in orbit, installed on celestial bodies, stationed in outer space in any other manner, and to air-, land-, or sea-based weapons capable of damaging or destroying satellites in orbit or entering orbit.

The basis for such an extension has already been suggested by United Nations action over the last twenty-five years.[20] Since 1981, the UN General Assembly has passed an annual resolution calling on all states to refrain from actions contrary to the peaceful uses of outer space and calling for negotiations within the UN Conference on Disarmament on an international agreement on the Prevention of an Arms Race in Outer Space (PAROS). Of the world's powers, only the United States and Israel have abstained on these resolutions, and in 2005, for the first time, the United States voted "No" on the PAROS Resolution.

In 1981, the Soviet Union also proposed a "Treaty on the Prohibition of the Stationing of Weapons of Any Kind in Outer Space." Since 1998, the Conference on Disarmament, due to a running dispute between the United States and China, has been deadlocked and unable to make any progress on what is now called the PAROS issue. The United States seeks a ban for fissile material for nuclear weapons (although without verification), but not a treaty on space weapons; the Chinese want to link negotiations of a treaty on fissile materials with a space treaty. Again, should there be a move toward diplomatic negotiation, this difference could be resolved.

In June of 2002, Russia and China, with several other states, jointly submitted a proposed treaty to the Conference on Disarmament to ban space weapons.[21] This move was particularly important, as resolutions are not binding, but treaties are. The treaty proposed by Russia and China would include obligations:

- Not to place in earthly orbit any objects carrying any kinds of weapons;
- Not to install such weapons on celestial bodies, or in outer space in any other manner;

- Not to resort to the threat or use of force against outer space objects; and
- Not to assist or encourage other States, groups of States, and international organizations to participate in activities banned by the Treaty.

Such activities have not been carried out by Russia since 1982, and China has not tested an anti-satellite device.[22] If China and Russia were really preparing the kind of Pearl Harbor that the Rumsfeld Commission spoke about, a clear test would be whether they would accept measures to enforce the treaty they have proposed. While such measures would need to be negotiated, they are clearly workable. In still another move to signal its willingness to de-weaponize space, on October 6, 2004, at the UN, Russia repeated its pledge not to be the first to deploy weapons in outer space and urged other countries to follow suit.

On June 9, 2005, Hu Xiaodi, China's chief negotiator, confirmed the statement of Dr. Hui Zhang at the "Full Spectrum Dominance" Conference, when he told the Disarmament Conference, "The recent developments concerning outer space are worrisome and require more urgent efforts to start work on preventing an arms race in outer space . . . China and Russia stand for the negotiation, at the Disarmament Conference, of an international legal instrument prohibiting the deployment of weapons in outer space and use of force against outer space objects." All three major parties—the United States, China, and Russia—would need to make concessions toward openness and enforcement to make such a treaty work. For example, the Chinese would probably have to drop their old objections that any satellite conducting military communications and targeting be included, as the time is probably past when such a provision could be supported by the United States. In any case, now is the time to start working on the solution of technical problems of enforcement, which could provide the basis of a treaty.

Clearly such a treaty, which the United States has rejected, most recently on June 13, 2006, at the Conference on Disarmament in Geneva,[23] is desired by our own citizens. A recent national poll conducted by the Program on International Policy Attitudes found that a treaty banning all weapons in space was considered a good idea by 74 percent of respondents, and only 21 percent favored building a missile defense system right away.[24] In an article titled "Space Sanctuary: A Viable National Strategy," Lt. Col. Bruce M. DeBlois, USAF, put the matter clearly: "The idea of putting weapons in space to dominate the globe is simply not compatible with who we are and what we represent as Americans."[25]

The United States remains the principal obstacle to an agreement. As Nancy Gallagher, the Associate Director for Research at the Center for International and Security Affairs at the University of Maryland, has pointed out, "The U.S. believes that it can have the best of both worlds—keep the protections that the Outer Space Treaty provides for peaceful space activities, while expanding U.S. military capabilities to control space for national advantage. Instead, it is likely to end up with the worst of both worlds where the U.S. stimulates threats and degrades international rules and institutions that offer some protection, without having the technical and financial means to actually achieve space dominance."

Gallagher asserts that a number of considerations keep the space community from taking any decisive action. One is that most commercial money accrues from satellites in geosynchronous orbit, which would be difficult to attack. Another is that a space war seems to many people to be sufficiently in the future that it can be discounted or ignored. Another is that because of the slump in spending on peaceful or commercial uses of space, there is a great deal of pressure from companies like Lockheed Martin and Boeing to go the military route.[26]

However, the responsibility of the U.S. government is to work for the benefit of its citizens, not a handful of well-connected military corporations. A space war, even if it were only likely ten or fifteen years from now, should be stopped now, while we have the opportunity, or it will be too late.

This reticence to act affects even action to prevent debris in space and to effectively allocate the radio spectrum and orbital slots. Theresa Hitchens writes: "Unfortunately, as with environmental issues here on Earth, while the need for a pollution-free, usable space environment is widely recognized, there continue to be disputes among space-faring powers about how best to address these issues. Part of the problem is the traditional bug-a-boo for environmental protection: preventative measures are best taken well in advance of a 'crisis,' but without the prospect of an immediate 'crisis,' most stakeholders are loath to take actions that could prove costly in the near term."[27] Here again, prudent action should be taken now to avoid disaster later. Is it wrong to expect such statesmanship from the U.S. government?

The larger issue of an arms race in outer space and a space war hangs over the world like the sword of Damocles. Diplomatic agreements should be pursued with vigor while we still have the option of acting. However, on January 24, 2002, John Bolton, then U.S. Undersecretary of State for Arms Control and Non-Proliferation, told the Conference for Disarmament that "the current international regime regulating the use of space meets all our purposes. We see no need for new agreements."[28]

Today, John Bolton is the U.S. Ambassador to the United Nations, and he has been replaced by Robert G. Joseph as Undersecretary of State for Arms Control and International Security Affairs, a man who, like Bolton, has dismissed arms control in favor of U.S. development and deployment of high-tech weapons. U.S. obstruction of international action to de-weaponize space has become an annual convention at the UN, which will probably continue as long as Bolton and others of his mind-set are making U.S. policy, although, under the increasing pressure created by the threat of space weaponization, and an active, engaged citizenry, this policy could change.

The move toward de-weaponization would be far from selfless. Both Russia and China have the ability to threaten U.S. space assets, and, particularly in the case of China, this ability would be tapped in any confrontation with the United States. In this sense, de-weaponization would be the most productive way of protecting our space assets, as opposed to weaponization.

Theresa Hitchens points out that "the future relationship between the United States and China will be a critical factor in determining whether space is weaponized." Useful diplomacy must replace rhetoric and bombast. "Today," she writes, "Washington and Beijing are engaged in a 'rhetorical' military competition in space, reminiscent of the 'mirror imaging' of worst-case assumptions about capability and intentions between the Cold War superpowers." Hitchens cites the Department of Defense's 2004 version of the Annual Report on the Military Power of the People's Republic of China which accuses China of "continuing efforts to investigate various means of tracking and defeating the space systems of potential opponents," and further charges that "China is clearly working on, and plans to field, ASATS [anti-satellite weapons] including ground-based laser and/or microsatellites." She also cites Dr. Gregory Kulack, a China expert at the Global Security Program of the Union of Concerned Scientists, who says China views U.S. plans for space "dominance as part of a larger U.S. strategy that includes preemptive war and specifically targets China as an enemy."[29]

This Cold War tone is played out in Pentagon war games where China is the opponent, constantly targeting U.S. space assets. Such games could become a self-fulfilling prophesy. Not only are the U.S. and Chinese military establishments not talking to each other about their growing hostility; the problem is compounded by secrecy and an increasing number of "China hawks" in the U.S.

military and civilian government. This very serious impasse could
change with a move toward productive diplomacy.

By 2004, China announced it would establish a manned space
station in earth orbit within fifteen years and was moving to put
men on the Moon. On October 12, 2005, China put two astronauts
into low-earth orbit for five days. One of the Chinese commenta-
tors remarked, "America's strategy is to lure China into a space race,
and to drain China's resources so it will collapse, without a war.
This is not a competition." President Hu stated, "China's space mission is solely based on peaceful purposes. We are devoted to the
peaceful use of space and are ready to extend our cooperation to
other countries."[30] However, China is now developing high resolution sensors which can be used for intelligence purposes, its own
satellite navigation system, and techniques to nullify U.S. space superiority through jamming and possible use of nuclear explosions
in space. The question whether the United States could protect its
space assets in wartime remains open. This is a situation calling for
common sense. It is clear that the United States must not weaponize
space but must negotiate a situation that voids the need to arm space
as a way of protecting its space assets.[31] Philip E. Coyle, Senior Advisor to the President of the Center for Defense Information, and
John B. Rhinelander, Vice President of Lawyers Alliance for World
Security (LAWS), remark, "Not since the development of the
atomic bomb has the United States had an equivalent opportunity
and incentive to show leadership for restraint in the development of
a new class of weapons, namely weapons in space."[32]

A WORLD TREATY BANNING SPACE-BASED WEAPONS

The text of a possible treaty was introduced into the U.S. House of
Representatives on October 2, 2001 by U.S. Congressman Dennis
J. Kucinich (D-Ohio), Co-Chair of the House Aviation and Space
Caucus. This treaty incorporates the wording and intention of the

1967 Outer Space Treaty, and of international proposals to ban space-based weapons and to preserve the cooperative, peaceful uses of outer space for all humankind.

The treaty has been presented to UN Secretary General Kofi Annan with a copy of the companion Space Preservation Act of 2002 (H.R. 3616).[33] This legislation would prohibit U.S. funds being spent on space-based weapons, end all research associated with such systems, and instruct the president to participate in international negotiations toward completion of a treaty banning space weapons worldwide. The treaty itself is ready to be signed, ratified, and passed into law.

The draft treaty would establish a permanent ban on all space-based weapons, implement a ban on the use of weapons to destroy or damage objects in space that are in orbit, and terminate research and development (R&D), testing, manufacturing, production, and deployment of all space-based weapons. It would also establish a vitally important outer space peacekeeping agency to monitor and enforce the permanent ban of *all* space-based weapons. This new treaty entity—the Outer Space Peacekeeping Agency—would have exclusive monitoring and enforcement jurisdiction in outer space to make it possible to achieve a ban on all space-based weapons and to preserve space for cooperative, peaceful purposes for the benefit of all humankind.[34]

Such a treaty would not have to go through the UN Conference on Disarmament where there might well be a three- to five-year process. The 1997 Land Mines Treaty Conference provides a successful precedent in which a specific subject matter—land mines—was addressed outside the UN Conference on Disarmament and was signed by 122 participating Member States through an international treaty conference, because it was so urgent.[35]

While no action has been taken on the Space Preservation Treaty, it remains a possible model. Citizen involvement will be necessary to convert drafts like the Space Preservation Treaty into reality.

The elements of this treaty are well known; the principal space powers, including China and Russia, are willing to go ahead; and time is running short. The United States is the only obstacle—Russia, China, and the EU nations are all ready to sign on to such a treaty, and make their views known every year in the UN. But the clock is ticking. Space weapons are on the drawing board, contracts are being made, and powerful interests are organizing around the possibility of a space arms race. The time to act is now—only an aroused U.S. public can achieve the de-weaponization of outer space.

A citizen-based organization, like the Global Network Against Weapons & Nuclear Power in Space with its 170 affiliates around the world, has the potential of organizing such a citizen movement. Director Bruce Gagnon has stated,

> People in these communities around the world, part of our global network, are saying we do not want our community to be used to participate in star wars, we didn't vote ourselves into this program, say our friends around the world, and we want out, and they are working to stop their country's participation in this program. . . . People are very interested in [the topic of weapons in space] because they understand that this will be the largest industrial project in the history of the planet Earth, necessitating cuts in education, in social security, in health care, and down the line. I call it pyramids to the heavens. The aerospace corporations are the pharaohs of our age, building these pyramids to the heavens and we, the taxpayers, will be the slaves.

"Why," Gagnon asks, "can't we use our hard earned tax dollars to build wind power and solar and fix our roads and bridges as the infrastructure of America crumbles? The time has come for a moral and ethical debate in the churches and in the classroom all across America around this question. . . . The time has come for us, as activists and humans to begin to see ourselves as one planet. You know when you . . . look at this planet it's nothing more than a little satellite passing through space, and we can thank the space program for that vision."[36]

The next few years will be crucial in stopping the weaponization of space. We must demand that our representatives represent us, not Boeing, Lockheed Martin, and all the other military corporations that fund the politicians. Your senators and representatives must work toward international cooperation in space. We must support with our hearts and souls candidates who are dedicated to diplomacy and a multilateral commitment to prevent war in heaven. We must join organizations dedicated to stopping the desecration of our universe by the weaponization of space.

The tools for this effort are already in place—the preliminary steps of cooperation, transparency, accountability; the rules of the road, and the drafts of treaties; as well as the support of the rest of the world. The United States must with urgency move away from its unilateral position, and join its co-habitants on this planet. This will happen only if we demand it!

Some Basic Information about Outer Space and Outer Space Weapons

Today the United States has 413 of the world's 795 satellites. The Russians, who follow the United States in total numbers, have 87. The Chinese have 34. The United States has approximately 135 military satellites and satellites which are listed as both military and civilian. The Russians have slightly over half their satellites in this category; the Chinese far fewer. Satellites are mostly in three orbits: (1) low-earth orbit [LEO] about 300 kilometers and up to a couple of thousand kilometers above the earth, which circle the earth in about an hour and a half to three hours (satellites presently in low-earth orbit are involved in high resolution imaging of the earth); (2) medium earth orbit [MEO] which go around the earth less frequently—these are the slots used by the Global Positioning System and navigation satellites; and (3) geosynchronous orbit [GEO], about 36,000 kilometers (22,300 miles) above the earth with a 24-hour orbit turning at the same rate as the earth. These are frequently communication and weather satellites.

Speeds in low-earth orbit are very high. A 747 jet travels at about 900 kilometers an hour, or a quarter of a kilometer a second. A satellite at 500 kilometers above the earth travels at 7.6 kilometers a second, or about 30 times faster. Because of the high speeds of orbiting objects, debris can be enormously destructive to satellites. As space is weaponized, the danger of debris increases, threatening the peaceful use of space for such things as positioning, communication, and weather mapping.

All satellites in the same orbit travel at the same speed. If you accelerate the satellite, it naturally moves into a different orbit, which makes it difficult for one satellite to maneuver so it can destroy another. As there is no air resistance, this change can only occur with a rocket thrust, which requires fuel and which is expensive to put into orbit. For example, to get a three-ton satellite from low-earth orbit to geosynchronous orbit requires nine tons of fuel. It takes about forty-five tons of fuel to put one ton of mass in orbit, which means that in addition to their high development costs, fuel costs (in addition, of course, to other launching costs) make space-based weapons very expensive in relation to earth-based weapons.

Once one knows the orbit of a satellite, it can be accurately tracked, and so is vulnerable to attack. A medium-range ballistic missile can knock out a satellite in low-earth orbit. Such a missile can be launched from the ground or the air. Also effective would be a nuclear explosion, which would create an electron belt that would injure all satellites passing through the belt. Knocking out satellites in geosynchronous orbit, which requires a trip of five hours, is clearly harder to do, either by a missile or by directed energy. Because space weapons are so vulnerable, they work best as first-strike systems, which makes their deployment highly threatening to world peace.[1]

Appendix 2

Treaty on Principles Governing the Activities of States in the Exploration and Use of Outer Space, Including the Moon and Other Celestial Bodies (The Outer Space Treaty of 1967)

The States Parties to this Treaty,

Inspired by the great prospects opening up before mankind as a result of man's entry into outer space,

Recognizing the common interest of all mankind in the progress of the exploration and use of outer space for peaceful purposes,

Believing that the exploration and use of outer space should be carried on for the benefit of all peoples irrespective of the degree of their economic or scientific development,

Desiring to contribute to broad international co-operation in the scientific as well as the legal aspects of the exploration and use of outer space for peaceful purposes,

Believing that such co-operation will contribute to the development of mutual understanding and to the strengthening of friendly relations between States and peoples,

Recalling resolution 1962 (XVIII), entitled "Declaration of Legal Principles Governing the Activities of States in the Exploration and Use of Outer Space," which was adopted unanimously by the United Nations General Assembly on 13 December 1963,

Recalling resolution 1884 (XVIII), calling upon States to refrain from placing in orbit around the earth any objects carrying nuclear weapons or any other kinds of weapons of mass destruction or from installing such weapons on celestial bodies, which was adopted unanimously by the United Nations General Assembly on 17 October 1963,

Taking account of United Nations General Assembly resolution 110 (II) of 3 November 1947, which condemned propaganda designed or likely to provoke or encourage any threat to the peace, breach of the peace or act of aggression, and considering that the aforementioned resolution is applicable to outer space,

Convinced that a Treaty on Principles Governing the Activities of States in the Exploration and Use of Outer Space, including the Moon and Other Celestial Bodies, will further the purposes and principles of the Charter of the United Nations,

Have agreed on the following:

ARTICLE I

The exploration and use of outer space, including the moon and other celestial bodies, shall be carried out for the benefit and in the interests of all countries, irrespective of their degree of economic or scientific development, and shall be the province of all mankind.

Outer space, including the moon and other celestial bodies, shall be free for exploration and use by all States without discrimination of any kind, on a basis of equality and in accordance with international law, and there shall be free access to all areas of celestial bodies.

There shall be freedom of scientific investigation in outer space, including the moon and other celestial bodies, and States shall facilitate and encourage international co-operation in such investigation.

ARTICLE II

Outer space, including the moon and other celestial bodies, is not subject to national appropriation by claim of sovereignty, by means of use or occupation, or by any other means.

ARTICLE III

States Parties to the Treaty shall carry on activities in the exploration and use of outer space, including the moon and other celestial bodies, in accordance with international law, including the Charter of the United Nations, in the interest of maintaining international peace and security and promoting international co-operation and understanding.

ARTICLE IV

States Parties to the Treaty undertake not to place in orbit around the earth any objects carrying nuclear weapons or any other kinds of weapons of mass destruction, install such weapons on celestial bodies, or station such weapons in outer space in any other manner.

The moon and other celestial bodies shall be used by all States Parties to the Treaty exclusively for peaceful purposes. The establishment of military bases, installations and fortifications, the testing of any type of weapons and the conduct of military manoeuvres on celestial bodies shall be forbidden. The use of military personnel for scientific research or for any other peaceful purposes shall not be prohibited. The use of any equipment or facility necessary for peaceful exploration of the moon and other celestial bodies shall also not be prohibited.

ARTICLE V

States Parties to the Treaty shall regard astronauts as envoys of mankind in outer space and shall render to them all possible assistance in the event of accident, distress, or emergency landing on the territory of another State Party or on the high seas. When astronauts make such a landing, they shall be safely and promptly returned to the State of registry of their space vehicle.

In carrying on activities in outer space and on celestial bodies, the astronauts of one State Party shall render all possible assistance to the astronauts of other States Parties.

States Parties to the Treaty shall immediately inform the other States Parties to the Treaty or the Secretary-General of the United Nations of any phenomena they discover in outer space, including the moon and other celestial bodies, which could constitute a danger to the life or health of astronauts.

ARTICLE VI

States Parties to the Treaty shall bear international responsibility for national activities in outer space, including the moon and other celestial bodies, whether such activities are carried on by governmental agencies or by non-governmental entities, and for assuring that national activities are carried out in conformity with the provisions set forth in the present Treaty. The activities of non-governmental entities in outer space, including the moon and other celestial bodies, shall require authorization and continuing supervision by the appropriate State Party to the Treaty. When activities are carried on in outer space, including the moon and other celestial bodies, by an international organization, responsibility for compliance with this Treaty shall be borne both by the international organization and by the States Parties to the Treaty participating in such organization.

ARTICLE VII

Each State Party to the Treaty that launches or procures the launching of an object into outer space, including the moon and other celestial bodies, and each State Party from whose territory or facility an object is launched, is internationally liable for damage to another State Party to the Treaty or to its natural or juridical persons by such object or its component parts on the Earth, in air or in outer space, including the moon and other celestial bodies.

ARTICLE VIII

A State Party to the Treaty on whose registry an object launched into outer space is carried shall retain jurisdiction and control over such object, and over any personnel thereof, while in outer space or on a celestial body. Ownership of objects launched into outer space, including objects landed or constructed on a celestial body, and of their component parts, is not affected by their presence in outer space or on a celestial body or by their return to the Earth. Such objects or component parts found beyond the limits of the State Party to the Treaty on whose registry they are carried shall be returned to that State Party, which shall, upon request, furnish identifying data prior to their return.

ARTICLE IX

In the exploration and use of outer space, including the moon and other celestial bodies, States Parties to the Treaty shall be guided by the principle of co-operation and mutual assistance and shall conduct all their activities in outer space, including the moon and other celestial bodies, with due regard to the corresponding interests of all other States Parties to the Treaty. States Parties to the Treaty shall pursue studies of outer space, including the moon and other celestial bodies, and conduct exploration of them so as to avoid their harmful contamination and also adverse changes in the environment of the Earth resulting from the introduction of extraterrestrial matter and, where necessary, shall adopt appropriate measures for this purpose. If a State Party to the Treaty has reason to believe that an activity or experiment planned by it or its nationals in outer space, including the moon and other celestial bodies, would cause potentially harmful interference with activities of other States Parties in the peaceful exploration and use of outer space, including the moon and other celestial bodies, it shall undertake appropriate international consultations before proceeding with any such activity or experiment. A State Party to the Treaty which has reason to believe that an activity or experiment planned by another State Party in outer space, including the moon and other celestial bodies, would cause potentially harmful interference with activities in the peaceful exploration and use of outer space, including the moon and other celestial bodies, may request consultation concerning the activity or experiment.

ARTICLE X

In order to promote international co-operation in the exploration and use of outer space, including the moon and other celestial bodies, in conformity with the purposes of this Treaty, the States Parties to the Treaty shall consider on a basis of equality any requests by other States Parties to the Treaty to be afforded an opportunity to observe the flight of space objects launched by those States. The nature of such an opportunity for observation and the conditions under which it could be afforded shall be determined by agreement between the States concerned.

ARTICLE XI

In order to promote international co-operation in the peaceful exploration and use of outer space, States Parties to the Treaty conducting activities in outer space, including the moon and other celestial bodies, agree to inform the Secretary-General of the United Nations as well as the public and the international scientific community, to the greatest extent feasible and practicable, of the nature, conduct, locations and results of such activities. On receiving the said information, the Secretary-General of the United Nations should be prepared to disseminate it immediately and effectively.

ARTICLE XII

All stations, installations, equipment and space vehicles on the moon and other celestial bodies shall be open to representatives of other States Parties to the Treaty on a basis of reciprocity. Such representatives shall give reasonable advance notice of a projected visit, in order that appropriate consultations may be held and that maximum precautions may be taken to assure safety and to avoid interference with normal operations in the facility to be visited.

ARTICLE XIII

The provisions of this Treaty shall apply to the activities of States Parties to the Treaty in the exploration and use of outer space, including the moon and other celestial bodies, whether such activities are carried on by a single State Party to the Treaty or jointly with other States, including cases where they are carried on within the framework of international intergovernmental organizations.

Any practical questions arising in connection with activities carried on by international intergovernmental organizations in the exploration and use of outer space, including the moon and other celestial bodies, shall be resolved by the States Parties to the Treaty either with the appropriate international organization or with one or more States members of that international organization, which are Parties to this Treaty.

ARTICLE XIV

1. This Treaty shall be open to all States for signature. Any State which does not sign this Treaty before its entry into

force in accordance with paragraph 3 of this article may accede to it at anytime.

2. This Treaty shall be subject to ratification by signatory States. Instruments of ratification and instruments of accession shall be deposited with the Governments of the United Kingdom of Great Britain and Northern Ireland, the Union of Soviet Socialist Republics and the United States of America, which are hereby designated the Depositary Governments.

3. This Treaty shall enter into force upon the deposit of instruments of ratification by five Governments including the Governments designated as Depositary Governments under this Treaty.

4. For States whose instruments of ratification or accession are deposited subsequent to the entry into force of this Treaty, it shall enter into force on the date of the deposit of their instruments of ratification or accession.

5. The Depositary Governments shall promptly inform all signatory and acceding States of the date of each signature, the date of deposit of each instrument of ratification of and accession to this Treaty, the date of its entry into force and other notices.

6. This Treaty shall be registered by the Depositary Governments pursuant to Article 102 of the Charter of the United Nations.

ARTICLE XV

Any State Party to the Treaty may propose amendments to this Treaty. Amendments shall enter into force for each State Party to the Treaty accepting the amendments upon their acceptance by a majority of the States Parties to the Treaty and thereafter for each remaining State Party to the Treaty on the date of acceptance by it.

ARTICLE XVI

Any State Party to the Treaty may give notice of its withdrawal from the Treaty one year after its entry into force by written notification to the Depositary Governments. Such withdrawal shall take effect one year from the date of receipt of this notification.

ARTICLE XVII

This Treaty, of which the English, Russian, French, Spanish and Chinese texts are equally authentic, shall be deposited in the archives of the Depositary Governments. Duly certified copies of this Treaty shall be transmitted by the Depositary Governments to the Governments of the signatory and acceding States.

IN WITNESS WHEREOF the undersigned, duly authorized, have signed this Treaty. DONE in triplicate, at the cities of London, Moscow and Washington, the twenty-seventh day of January, one thousand nine hundred and sixty-seven.

Notes

Preface

1. www.ostp.gov/html/us%20National%20space%20policy.pdf.

2. "Report on e-Parliament Conference on Space Security," September 14, 2005, 2105 Rayburn-ouse Office Building, Washington, DC.

1. A Brief History of Outer Space

1. "Implementing Our Vision for Space Control," speech by General Richard B. Meyers, United States Space Foundation, Colorado Springs, April 7, 1999.

2. See "The Internal Space Race," Illinois Institute of Technology, http://www.gl.itt.edu/wadc/History/space race. In recent years, the NASA budget has shrunk to a small fraction of its original size. For example, in 2000, it was less than a fifth in adjusted dollars of what the United States spent on the Apollo program alone. The Russian civil outer space program has shrunk even more drastically. *Space Security 2003*, the Eisenhower Institute, 2004, p. 83. Nevertheless, with a budget of $16.5 billion, NASA is still the world's largest civil space investor. Space Security 2006, Executive Summary, sestabrooks@plowshares.ca.

3. For an early overview of the history of cooperation in outer space, see Walter A. McDougall, *The Heavens and the Earth: A Political History of the Space Age* (Basic Books, 1985).

4. Two weeks later, President Kennedy initiated four specific proposals which included (1) the establishment of an operational world weather satellite system through the coordinated launching of U.S. and Soviet weather satellites; (2) the exchange of spacecraft tracking services, each side providing the equipment to be operated on the other's territory by the other's technicians; (3) the mapping of the earth's magnetic field with satellites from both countries in complementary

orbits; and (4) the joint testing of intercontinental communication satellites. For a detailed description of early cooperation between the United States and the Soviet Union, see Arnold W. Frutkin, *International Cooperation in Space* (Prentice Hall, 1965), chapter 3.

5. The primary reason, for example, that the Soviet Union backed down during the Cuban Missile Crisis in October 1962, and agreed to dismantle its missiles in Cuba, is that the United States had already established a clear missile superiority. In an ultimate showdown, the United States could deliver up to seven times as much explosive power as the Soviet Union, although the cost to the United States of a nuclear exchange would still be cataclysmic. See *The Cuban Missile Crisis: Selected Foreign Policy Documents from the Administration of John F. Kennedy, January 1961–November 1962* (The Stationery Office, 2001).

6. Federation of American Scientists, "Ensuring America's Space Security: Report of the FAS Panel on Weapons in Space," August 2004, pp. 8–9, relying on a report of Albert Wheelon, then Deputy Director of the CIA.

7. Michael Krepon and Christopher Clary, *Space Assurance or Space Dominance? The Case Against Weaponizing Space* (The Henry L. Stimson Center, 2003), p. 20.

8. Helen Caldicott, *Missile Envy* (William Morrow, 1984).

9. Despite such cooperation, and the enormous excitement it generated, the IGY never could get completely beyond either the military competition between the United States and the Soviet Union or the underlying problem of nationalism. Dr. James Van Allen, the discoverer of the radiation belts surrounding the earth, which now bear his name, expressed his doubts that the IGY would overcome the intense military rivalry which was clearly signaled in outer space. Creating laws for outer space might not work. "Both practically and diplomatically," he said, "this is a very fine undertaking, but it is not at all clear how such arrangements can be managed if space is a military undertaking." Hearings before the Select Committee on Astronautics and Space Exploration, 85th Congress, Second Session on H.R. 11881, p. 871. While scientific institutions did cooperate in the International Geophysical Year, even in this purely scientific enterprise, there was no significant integration of government programs. See Arnold W. Frutkin, *International Cooperation in Space* (Prentice Hall, 1965).

10. Negotiation of this treaty had begun in 1953, with the United States insisting on on-site inspections of nuclear facilities, and the Soviets seeking a moratorium on testing without any inspection. This disagreement had been at the core of the breakdown in negotiations on the Baruch Plan, proposed by the United States following World War II, to control nuclear weapons, before the Soviet

Union had developed its own nuclear bomb in 1949. After seemingly endless negotiations, agreement was finally reached on what became the Limited Test Ban in 1963, which may well have been facilitated by the danger of a nuclear exchange during the preceding Cuban Missile Crisis.

11. Personal experience of Craig Eisendrath, at the time handling the multilateral aspects of the U.S. outer space program in the UN Political Office of the U.S. State Department.

12. Although China and Iran have announced their support for the 1967 Outer Space Treaty, it is important to note that they have not yet formally ratified it.

13. Other agreements have added to this growing body of international law, such as the 1988 Ballistic Missile Launch Notification Agreement between the United States and the Soviet Union, which provides for notification, no less than 24 hours in advance of the launch, of the planned date, launch area, and area of impact for any launch of an intercontinental ballistic missile or a submarine-launched ballistic missile. Agreements such as these could be extended to outer space launches as well.

14. For a thorough review of all existing disarmament agreements that mandate or suggest extension into outer space, see Michael Krepon with Christopher Clary, *Space Assurance or Space Dominance? The Case Against Weaponizing Space* (The Henry L. Stimson Center, 2003), pp. 91–101.

15. Richard P. Hallion, "Precision Guided Munitions and the New Era of Warfare," Air Power Studies Centre, 18 October 2000.

16. "Full Spectrum Dominance" Conference, Airlie House, May 16–17, 2005.

17. In March of 2005, the NATO Council, in fact, agreed to cooperate on an active, layered, theater ballistic missile defense to protect troops on the battlefield from short-range ballistic missiles. The system is expected to be operational in 2012. This arrangement, however, may be jeopardized by the Bush administration's plans to deploy weapons in space. Still another problem is that by sharing missile defense technology, the United States is also providing the same technology that is used to launch missiles, and is thereby encouraging missile proliferation.

18. This primitive system is inadequate to stop a launch from Russia, because Russia maintains over a thousand nuclear-armed missiles aimed at the United States on hair-trigger alert, so it could simply overwhelm the missile defense system by sheer numbers. China, however, has said that it will increase the number of its ICBMs aimed at the United States so that its deterrence capacity is not threatened by any missile defense system the United States installs—it has presently only about twenty ICBMs aimed at the United States. Ironically, the U.S. system,

presently installed in Alaska and California, which is designed to knock down anti-ballistic missiles, has only eleven anti-missile devices (nine in Alaska and two in California) and does not work. It has failed numerous tests, and it is useless against decoys.

2. The Peaceful Potential of Outer Space

1. Keith Hall, speech to National Space Club, September 15, 1997.

2. "Weapons of Terror: Freeing the World of Nuclear, Biological and Chemical Arms," Report of the Weapons of Mass Destruction Commission, EO Grafiska, Stockholm, May 2006.

3. One factor that has made increasing commercial use of outer space possible is the declining cost of space launches. While in 1990, a launch of a communication satellite cost $40,000 per kilogram, in 2000, this had gone down to $26,000 per kilogram. Simon Collard-Wexler, Jessy Cowan-Sharp, Sarah Estabrooks, Amb. Thomas Graham Jr., Dr. Robert Lawson, and Dr. William Marshall, *Space Security 2004* (Northview Press), p. xiii.

4. "NASA Spinoffs: Bringing Space Down to Earth," *The Ultimate Space Page*, available at http://www.thespaceplace.com/nasa/spinoffs.html, cited by *Space Security 2003* (The Eisenhower Institute, 2004), p. 87.

5. INTELSAT entered into force in 1973. As Nancy Gallagher points out, for the first five years of this project, the U.S. firms got all the business. The Soviet Union refused to participate. The U.S. efforts to use its monopoly to launch services for Western countries to protect its dominant position in INTELSAT had the unintended effect of spurring the Europeans to develop independent satellite manufacturing and launch capabilities. "The Peaceful Uses of Outer Space (1957–2005): Environmental and Weather Observation, Communications, Arms Control, and Global Economics," "Full Spectrum Dominance" Conference, Airlie House, May 16–17, 2005.

6. A second decade of satellite technology has established the International Maritime Satellite Organization (INMARSAT), which provides multiple global satellite systems beyond INTELSAT. On July 18, 2001, INTELSAT became a private company, which owns and manages a constellation of communication satellites that provide international broadcast services, and is funded through usage fees. Today INTELSAT is facing increasing competitive pressure from other systems.

7. See COSPAS-SARSAT—National Search and Rescue Secretariat, http://www.nss.gc.ca/site/cospas-sarsat/index_e.asp.

8. See "COSPAS-SARSAT Rescues as of September 9, 2005," NOAA Satellite and Information Service, http://www.sarsat.noaa.gove/sarsast.html.

9. Errors are caused by a number of factors, including inaccurate clocks in the receivers, and differences in the speed of light as it goes through different atmospheric conditions, which sometimes amount to over 10 meters of inaccuracy.

10. "ILRS Home, Satellite Missions, List of Satellites, Jason-1," ilrs.gsfc.nasa.gov/satellite_missions/list_of_satellites/jason/index/html.

11. Satellites also gauged the effectiveness of strikes; navigation satellites led U.S. ships to their deployment areas; and communication satellites passed command and control information between military leaders and strikes forces. "Military Space Operations: Desert Shield/Storm," http://www.fas.org/spp/military/docops/operate. See also "Navstar Global Positioning System," GlobalSecurity.org, http://www.globalsecurity.org/space/systems/gps.htm.

12. Federation of American Scientists, *Ensuring America's Space Security: Report of the FAS Panel on Weapons in Space*, August 2004, p. 35. As the United States also relies heavily on commercial satellites, in 1992 it passed a law prohibiting taking pictures of certain areas if it would compromise national security. Michael Krepon with Christopher Clary, *Space Assurance or Space Dominance? The Case Against Weaponizing Space* (The Henry L. Stimson Center, 2003), pp. 16–17.

13. Simon Collard-Wexler, Jessy Cowan-Sharp, Sarah Estabrooks, Ambassador Thomas Graham Jr., Dr. Robert Lawson, and Dr. William Marshall, *Space Security 2004* (Northview Press), p. 124; the quotation is from the Office of Science and Technology Policy, "U.S. Space-Based Positioning, Navigation, and Timing Policy," Fact Sheet, December 15, 2004, http://www.ostp.gov/html/FactSheetSPACE-BASEDPOSITIONINGNAVIGATIONTIMING,pdf.

14. "Global Positioning System Overview," developed by Peter H. Dana, Department of Geography, University of Texas at Austin, revised May 1, 2000, www.colorado.edu/geography/gcraft/notes/gps/gps.html.

15. The European Commission estimates that Galileo will benefit the European economy by creating more than 100,000 jobs. In 2005, the European Commission announced its plan to spend more than $5 billion on "Security and Space" programs from 2006 to 2013, and to double its budget for space-related research programs. *Space Security 2006 Report*, Executive Summary, sestabrooks@plowshares.ca. For the role of the European Commission, see Daniel Keohane, *Europe in Space*, Centre for European Reform, October 2004.

16. *GPS World*; see also Galileo Position System, wikipedia.org/wiki/Galileo_positioning_system.

17. Tomas Valasek, "Galileo's 'Strategic' Role," *Europe in Space*, Centre for European Reform, October 2004.

18. Simon Collard-Wexler, Jessy Cowan-Sharp, Sarah Estabrooks, Ambassador

Thomas Graham Jr., Dr. Robert Lawson, and Dr. William Marshall, *Space Security 2004* (Northview Press), p. 59.

19. *Space Security 2003*, The Eisenhower Institute, 2004, pp. 68–69.

20. For example, the shift from Newtonian physics to the field theory of Clerk Maxwell provided the physical basis for the philosophy and psychology of William James, and the therapeutic work of Harry Stack Sullivan. For a discussion of the connection between scientific models and other aspects of thought, see Craig Eisendrath, *At War with Time: The Wisdom of Western Thought from the Sages to a New Activism for Our Time* (Helios Press, 2003), chapters 7–9.

21. "A Renewed Spirit of Discovery," White House, January 14, 2004. See also "Science and Space: Bush Unveils Vision for Moon and Beyond," CNN.com, January 15, 2004.

22. *Washington Post*, January 15, 2004.

23. "Science and Space: Bush Unveils Vision for Moon and Beyond," CNN.com, January 15, 2004. CNN reports that "NASA will begin sending a series of robotic missions to the moon beginning in 2008 to conduct research and prepare for future missions, and research will be conducted on the space station on the long-term effects of extended space travel on human physiology."

24. "The Moon-Mars Program, http://www.aura-astronomy.org/nv/APS_Report.pdf.

25. Dennis Overbye, "Much-Promoted NASA Missions Would Be Threatened Under Agency's Budget," *New York Times*, March 2, 2006.

26. *Washington Post*, April 10, 2005.

27. On March 27, 2006, Guy Gugliotta of the *Washington Post* reported that since Bush's 2004 "Vision for Space Exploration," "mishaps and delays with the space shuttle and the space station programs have shrunk both the moon research budget and the rhetoric promoting the mission."

3. Missile Defense

1. Lance W. Lord, General, USAF Commander, Foreword, *Strategic Master Plan FY04 and Beyond*.

2. On March 20, 2006, Bob Brewin of FederalComputerWeekly.com reported, "After an audit [released earlier in the month], the IG [Inspector General] concluded that the MDA [Missile Defense Agency] 'had not completed a systems engineering plan or planned fully for system sustainment,' the report states. 'Therefore, the [MDA] is at risk of not successfully developing an integrated ballistic missile defense system.'"

3. For a history of missile defense, see Craig Eisendrath, Melvin A. Goodman,

and Gerald E. Marsh, *The Phantom Defense: America's Pursuit of the Star Wars Illusion* (Praeger, 2001), chapter 1. See also Frances Fitzgerald, *Way Out There in the Blue: Reagan, Star Wars and the End of the Cold War* (Simon & Schuster, 2000), which documents the early efforts to influence missile defense through lobbying; William J. Broad, *Teller's War: The Top Secret Story Behind the Star Wars Deception* (Simon & Schuster, 1992); and Janne E. Nolan, *Guardians of the Arsenal: The Politics of Nuclear Strategy* (Basic Books, 1989).

4. Richard L. Garwin, Reed Senior Fellow for Science and Technology at the Council on Foreign Relations, also speaks of "100 or 200 little bomblets" of anthrax which could survive reentry through the atmosphere, which would totally confuse a missile defense system. "Full Spectrum Dominance" Conference, Airlie House, May 16–17, 2005.

5. The United States actually installed its one permitted missile defense site in Grand Forks, North Dakota, at a cost of $6 billion, only to dismantle it immediately when it became clear it would be ineffective. The Soviets deployed a limited missile defense system, using nuclear-tipped interceptors, around Moscow, which U.S. military planners called *Galosh* and discounted as ineffective, but which appears to continue to have nuclear explosives.

6. Teller saw himself as man with a mission who could save the United States from the communists, without realizing that his enthusiasm often outran the practicality of some of his schemes. See Edward Teller's *Memoirs: A Twentieth Century Journey in Science and Politics*, by Edward Teller with Judith Shoolery (Perseus, 2001); see also Craig Eisendrath, "The Life and Physics of Edward Teller," *Baltimore Sun*, November 4, 2001.

7. Strobe Talbott, *Master of the Game* (Knopf, 1988), cited by Craig Eisendrath, Melvin A. Goodman, and Gerald E. Marsh, in *The Phantom Defense: America's Pursuit of the Star Wars Illusion* (Praeger, 2001), pp. 17–18.

8. Hartung writes that a key lobbying organization has been the Center for Security Policy, whose board has included Senator Jon L. Kyl (R-AZ) and Representative Curt Weldon (R-PA). Corporate executives from Lockheed Martin have served on the board of the Center for Security Policy, as well as representatives from major conservative think tanks like Power America and the Heritage Foundation. Hartung also points out that the industry gave George W. Bush almost five times as much as it gave Al Gore in the 2000 campaign, and that in the second Rumsfeld Commission on National Security Uses in Space, seven of thirteen commissioners had former or current ties to the aerospace industry. In addition, a number of key figures in the Bush administration have been drawn from the aerospace industry; significantly, Vice President Cheney is a former member of the board of TRW,

which was one of the major contractors. "Full Spectrum Dominance" Conference, Airlie House, May 16–17, 2005. See also William D. Hartung with Frida Berrigan, Michelle Ciarrocca, and Jonathan Wingo, "Tangled Web 2005: A Profile of the Missile Defense Space Weapons Lobbies," World Policy Institute–Arms Trade Resource Center, www.worldpolicy.org/projects/arms/reports/tangledweb.html, and Hartung's *How Much Are You Making on the War, Daddy? A Quick and Dirty Guide to War Profiteering in the Bush Administration* (Nation Books, 2003).

9. Reported by Karl Grossman in "Star Wars: Protecting Globalization from Above," January 18, 2002, 222.corpwatch.org/issues/PID.jsp?articleid=1333.

10. "Report of the Commission to Assess the Ballistic Missile Threat to the United States," National Intelligence Council, "National Intelligence Estimate (NIE), Foreign Missile Development and the Ballistic Missile Threat to the United States through 2015," unclassified summary, September 1999.

11. "Full Spectrum Dominance" Conference, Airlie House, May 16–17, 2005.

12. Joseph Cirincione, "The Declining Ballistic Missile Threat," presented at the American Association for the Advancement of Science Annual Meeting and Science Innovation Exposition, Boston, Massachusetts, February 18, 2002.

13. This conclusion was essentially reiterated by the public 2000 National Intelligence Estimate.

14. Joseph Cirincione, "Assessing the Assessment: The 1999 National Intelligence Estimate of the Ballistic Missile Threat," *The Nonproliferation Review*, Spring 2000.

15. As Ambassador Thomas Graham points out, "With the attack . . . on the World Trade Center and the Pentagon with highjacked air-liners, the political imperative of missile defense became almost irresistible. Some administration spokesmen argued that this attack proved the necessity of missile defense. In mid-September 2001, a senior administration official was reported as saying that 'these people had jet plane pilots. And if these same people had access to ballistic missiles, do you think they wouldn't have used them?' In the United States, this argument was accepted to a degree, though it is precisely the wrong message to take from the September 11 attacks. The attack was low-tech, not high-tech. . . . Terrorist organizations, the principal threat to national security today, have never shown the slightest interest in ballistic missiles." "Full Spectrum Dominance" Conference, Airlie House, May 16–17, 2005.

16. See Craig Eisendrath, "Suing the President," *USA Today Magazine*, May 2003.

17. "ABM Treaty Suit Dismissed," CNN.com./law center, December 31, 2002. On February 13, 2003, six members of the House, joined by members of

the military and parents of service personnel, filed a lawsuit seeking to prevent President Bush from invading Iraq without an explicit declaration of war from Congress. Here, members of the House went to the courts, again unsuccessfully, to affirm congressional powers being challenged by the president.

18. Sam Bishop, "More Work Set For Greeley," *Fairbanks Daily News-Miner*, February 5, 2006. See also Matthew Hoey, "Military Space Systems: The Road Ahead," Institute for Defense and Disarmament Studies, October 22, 2005, p. 13; and Jeremy Singer, "Obering Defends Missile Defense System, Belittles Agency's Critics, *Space News*, March 27, 2006. Air Force Lt. Gen. Henry Obering is the director of the Missile Defense Agency.

19. Even if North Korea, the most likely candidate, were to develop ICBM capacity, would such a ground-based missile defense be the most effective? On the contrary, Richard Garwin, IBM Fellow Emeritus at the Watson Research Center, makes clear that a system of rockets located on ships near North Korea and others installed with Russian cooperation near North Korea, would be more effective in intercepting their ICBMs. "Full Spectrum Dominance" Conference, Airlie House, May 16–17, 2005. See also his "Space Weapons and the Risk of Accidental Nuclear War," Arms Control Association, December 2005. Recent tests indicate increased effectiveness of ship-based missile defense systems. Taylor Dinerman, "Missile Defense in 2006: Now More Controversial than Ever," *The Space Review*, January 30, 2006.

20. Tony Capaccio, "Missile Defense Gets Faint Praise from U.S. Tester," *Bloomberg News Service*, January 19, 2006.

21. David Ruppe, "Annual U.S. Missile Defense Spending Could Double," *Global Security Newswire*, January 24, 2006. The report also says that if the Defense Department chooses to deploy no additional missile defense systems, and only spends on research and development, annual costs could go down to $3 billion through 2024. See also Lt. Gen. Robert Gard (USA, Ret.) and John Isaacs, "Stop Deployment of National Missile Defense," Council for a Livable World, February 8, 2006. Efforts to drastically cut the missile budget have failed.

22. "Pentagon Report: Bush Missile Defense of Questionable Quality," Council for a Livable World, February 25, 2003, www.clw.org.

23. The Council for a Livable World has maintained a running account of the strategic issues involved in missile defense at www.clw.org.

24. Will Durham, "US Makes Missile Defense System Operational," *Reuters*, June 20, 2006.

25. Despite the problems of the missile defense system, President Bush still said, "Yes, I think we had a reasonable chance of shooting it down. At least that's

what the military commanders told me." Transcript of President Bush's News Conference, *New York Times*, July 7, 2006.

26. At issue from the North Korean side is help in meeting famine, energy supplies, access to communication satellites, taking mines out of the demilitarized zone, ending the Korean War, and some assurance of nonaggression; from the U.S. side, North Korean renunciation of nuclear weapons and acceptance of intrusive inspections.

27. Hari Kumar and David E. Sanger, "India Reports a Long-Range Missile Test," *New York Times*, July 10, 2006.

28. In late 2005, Iran's leadership, including President Amedinajad, began making statements that threatened the very existence of Israel.

29. Marin Sieff, "BMD Watch: Arrow Can Blast Shihabs," *UPI*, March 9, 2006.

30. Liz Sidoti, "Frist: European Missile-Defense Site Needed," *Associated Press*, June 30, 2006.

31. Michael R. Gordon, "U.S. Is Proposing European Shield for Iran Missiles, *New York Times*, May 22, 2006.

32. Dr. Kurt Gottfried, "UCS Statement on Iran and Nuclear Threats," April 17, 2006, http://lists101.his.com/mailman/listinto/nwwg.

33. This issue was discussed by Loring Wirbel, Communications Editorial Director, Communication Systems Design and CMP Media LLC, at the "Full Spectrum Dominance" Conference, Airlie House, May 16–17, 2005. See also his *Star Wars: US Tools of Space Supremacy* (Pluto Press, distributed by University of Michigan Press, 2003).

34. Craig Eisendrath, Melvin A. Goodman, and Gerald E. Marsh, *The Phantom Defense: America's Pursuit of the Star Wars Illusion* (Prometheus, 2001), p. 131.

35. "Full Spectrum Dominance" Conference, Airlie House, May 16–17, 2005.

36. Carah Ong, Washington, DC Office Director, Nuclear Age Peace Foundation, March 22, 2006. For additional polling information, see Ann Roosevelt, "MDA Poised to Expand the Initial Missile Defense Capability," *Defense Daily*, March 22, 2006.

37. By January 2006, the missile defense system had not staged any intercept tests for almost a year following two failed tests. "US Stages Missile Defense 'War Games' for Congress," *Reuters*, January 24, 2006. David Ruppe, *Global Security Newswire*, October 7, 2005 and January 12, 2006.

4. The Weaponization of Outer Space

1. U.S. Air Force Advisory Board, "New World Vistas: Air and Space Power for the 21st Century," *Space Technology*, 1996.

2. "Vision for 2020," U.S. Space Command, April 1997. See also "Long Range Plan: Implementing the USSPACECOM Vision for 2020," U.S. Space Command, April 1998.

3. Quoted by Michael Moore, in his address, "Space Control: A Very Old Idea" at the "Full Spectrum Dominance" Conference, Airlie House, May 16–17, 2005.

4. Ibid.

5. "Vision 2020," released in 1997, has been updated by a new Air Force Vision document, "Lasting Heritage . . . Limitless Horizons: A Warfighter's Vision," released on February 28, 2006.

6. *Report of the Commission to Assess United States National Security Space Management and Organization,* January 11, 2001.

7. See "Counterspace Operations," Air Force Doctrine Document 2-2-1, United States Air Force, August 2, 2004, p. 2, and *Joint Publication 3-14,* cited by Simon Collard-Wexler, Jessy Cowan-Sharp, Sarah Estabrooks, Ambassador Thomas Graham Jr., Dr. Robert Lawson, and Dr. William Marshall, *Space Security 2004* (Northview Press), p. 38.

8. Karl P. Mueller, "Is the Weaponization of Space Inevitable?" Paper delivered at the International Studies Association Annual Convention, March 27, 2002, p. 4ff, cited by Michael Krepon with Christopher Clary, *Space Assurance or Space Dominance: The Case Against Weaponizing Space* (The Henry L. Stimson Center, 2003), p. 40.

9. Tim Weiner, "Air Force Seeks Bush's Approval for Space Weapons Programs," *New York Times,* May 18, 2005.

10. Jeffrey Richelson, "The Satellite Gap," *Bulletin of the Atomic Scientists* (January–February, 2003), pp. 49–50, cited by Michael Krepon with Christopher Clary, *Space Assurance or Space Dominance?: The Case Against Weaponizing Space,* p. 13.

11. Prepared Testimony on Ballistic Missile Defense to the Senate Armed Services Committee, July 12, 2001.

12. Victoria Samson, research analyst, Center for Defense Information, "An 'F' for Missile Defense: How seven government reports in two months illustrate the need for missile defense to change its ways," March 2006. See also Andrea Shalai-Esa, "Auditors Fault Missile Defense Plans," *Reuters,* June 1, 2006.

13. Martin Sieff, "Boost Phase Blues Impact Missile Shield Developments," *UPI,* June 16, 2006.

14. David Ruppe, *Global Security Newswire,* February 3, 2006.

15. Bryan Bender, "Pentagon Eyeing Weapons in Space: Budget Seeks Millions to Test New Technologies," *Boston Globe,* March 14, 2006; see also Gopal Ratnam, "Command Not Yet Set for U.S. Missile Shield," *Defense News,* March 27, 2006. See also Union of Concerned Scientists, Global Security, www.ucsusa.org/

global_security/space_weapons; and Ivan Safranchuk, "The Link Between Missile Defense and Space Weaponization," Bulletin 20—Prevention of an Arms Race in Outer Space, International Network of Engineers and Scientists Against Proliferation, www.inesap.org/bulletin20/bul20art05.htm.

16. Jeremy Singer, *Space News*, April 18, 2005.

17. Noah Shachtman, "Pentagon Preps for War in Space," February 20, 2004, http://www.wired.com/news/technology/0,1282,62358,00/html. See also William J. Broad, "Administration Conducting Research into Laser Weapons," *New York Times*, May 3, 2006.

18. See "Space-Based Infrared System," www.sbirslowteam.com; and "Space-Based Infrared System—High," www.lockheedmartin.com/wms/findPage.do? dsp=fec&ci-11497&rsbci=0&fti=126.

19. Ibid. See also Lt. Gen. Robert Gard (USA, Ret.) and John D. Isaacs, Center for Arms Control and Non-Proliferation, "The Illusion of Operational Readiness of National Missile Defense," July 2006.

20. Theresa Hitchens, March 2, 2006, nwwg-bounces@lists101.his.com. Theresa Hitchens, Michael Kaz-Hyman, and Victoria Samson report on three experiments that will be conducted in support of the Space-Based Interceptor Test Bed: "(l) distributed sensing by two or three microsatellites; (2) a propulsion experiment believed to be the classified Microsatellite Propulsion Experiment (MPX) designed to test space-based interception technologies; and (3) Target Risk-Reduction Experiment using a miscrosatellite as a target for ballistic missile interceptors." "Space Weapons Could Emerge from Pentagon Budget," The Henry L. Stimson Center, March 7, 2006.

21. Russian Federation Statement to the 2002 Non-Proliferation Committee, April 8, 2002, cited by David Grahame, "A Question of Intent: Missile Defense and the Weaponization of Space," in *Basic Notes*, May 1, 2002.

22. Tim Weiner, "Air Force Seeks Bush's Approval for Space Weapons Program," *New York Times*, May 18, 2005.

23. Simon Collard-Wexler, Jessy Cowan-Sharp, Sarah Estabrooks, Ambassador Thomas Graham Jr., Dr. Robert Lawson, and Dr. William Marshall, *Space Security 2004* (Northview Press), p. 123.

24. Tim Weiner, "Air Force Seeks Bush's Approval for Space Weapons Program," *New York Times*, May 18, 2005.

25. *Space Security 2006*, Executive Summary.

26. Jeremy Singer writes of the development of laser anti-satellite weapons despite the fact that "the Air Force Research Laboratory says it is not developing such weapons. 'The language in the research budget justification was simply

intended to reflect possible future applications of this technology and was not an indication of Air Force efforts in the area of anti-satellite weapons,' said Eva Blaylock, a spokeswoman for the lab's directed energy department. . . . The laboratory is primarily interested in improving laser technology for use in keeping tabs on objects in space, and has 'no plans to develop or field an anti-satellite demonstration or operational system,' Blaylock said in an April 27 [2006] written response to questions, cited by Singer." Singer, however, writes that Theresa Hitchens "said the wording in the budget justification materials seemed to suggest otherwise. Pentagon documents are generally worded very carefully, making it strange that the military would label anti-satellite technology as the first on a list of possible applications for experiments if it was not pursuing such weapons." "USAF Interest in Lasers Triggers Concerns About Anti-Satellite Weapons," *Space News*, May 2, 2006.

27. Simon Collard-Wexler, Jessy Cowan-Sharp, Sarah Estabrooks, Ambassador Thomas Graham Jr., Dr. Robert Lawson, and Dr. William Marshall, *Space Security 2004* (Northview Press), p. xix.

28. Tim Weiner, "Air Force Seeks Bush's Approval for Space Weapons Program," *New York Times*, May 18, 2005. See also Giuseppe Anzera, "The Pentagon's Bid to Militarize Space," *Globalvision News Network*, August 17, 2005; and Matthew Hoey, Research Associate, Institute for Defense and Disarmament Studies, "Military Space Systems: The Road Ahead," October 22, 2005, p. 9. Hoey reports that the DART (Demonstration of Autonomous Rendezvous Technology) spacecraft, launched on April 15, 2005, showed similar capabilities, with similar possibilities to become an anti-satellite weapon.

29. Federation of American Scientists, "Ensuring America's Space Security: Report on the FAS Panel on Weapons in Space," August 2004, pp. 16–19.

30. David Barton et al., "Report of the APS Study Group on Boost-Phase Intercept Systems for National Missile Defense," American Physical Society, July 15, 2003, cited by Simon Collard-Wexler, Jessy Cowan-Sharp, Sarah Estabrooks, Ambassador Thomas Graham Jr., Dr. Robert Lawson, and Dr. William Marshall, *Space Security 2004* (Northview Press), p. 144. See also William D. Hartung with Frida Berrigan, Michelle Ciarrocca, and Jonathan Wingo, "Tangled Web 2005: A Profile of the Missile Defense and Space Weapons Lobbies," World Policy Institute, www.worldpolicy.org/projects/arms/reports/tangledweb.html.

31. *Space Security 2004*, pp. 102, 121, and 128.

32. Michael Krepon with Christopher Clary, *Space Assurance or Space Dominance: The Case Against Weaponizing Space* (The Henry L. Stimson Center, 2003), p. 75. For an excellent description of defensive measures, see pp. 68–75.

33. For details, see "Space Weapons Spending in FY 06, Presidential Request," Center for Defense Information, February 11, 2005. As with other outer space weapons, the spending on such systems is extremely difficult to track, as it is hidden in ambiguous areas of the budgets of the U.S. Air Force, Missile Defense Agency, and Defense Advanced Research Projects Agency.

34. "Full Spectrum Dominance" Conference, Airlie House, May 16–17, 2005. See also Giuseppe Anzera, "The Pentagon's Bid to Militarize Space," Globalvision News Network, August 17, 2005.

35. Ibid.

36. Walter Pincus, "Pentagon Has Far-Reaching Defense Spacecraft in Works," *Washington Post*, March 16, 2005, www.washingtonpost.com/ac2/wp-dyn/A38272-2005Mar15. See also Matthew Hoey, "Military Space Systems: The Road Ahead," Institute for Defense and Disarmament Studies, October 22, 2005, pp. 14–15.

37. Giuseppe Anzera, "The Pentagon's Bid to Militarize Space," Power and Interest News Report, August 17, 2005.

38. Quoted by Tim Weiner, "Air Force Seeks Bush's Approval for Space Weapons Program," *New York Times*, May 18, 2005.

39. The Bush administration has undertaken to rebuild the nation's aging nuclear weapons complex, which would include restoring the U.S. capacity to manufacture large-scale nuclear bombs. Up to now the country has relied on bombs produced during the Cold War. The move has been criticized because it would encourage aspiring nuclear powers to develop their own weapons. See Ralph Vartabedian, "U.S. Rolls Out Nuclear Plan: The administration's proposal would modernize the nation's complex of laboratories and factories as well as produce new bombs," *Los Angeles Times*, April 6, 2006. See also "Interim Report on the Feasibility and Implementation of the Reliable Replacement Warhead Program: Submitted to the Congressional Defense Committees in Response to Section 3111 of the National Authorization Act for Fiscal Year 2006, Public Law 109-163, by the Secretaries of Defense and Energy in Consultation with the Nuclear Weapons Council," March 1, 2006. See also David Ruppe, "Lawmaker Warns Against New U.S. Nukes," *Global Security Newswire*, March 31, 2006.

40. *The Strategic Master Plan FY06 of the Air Force Space Command*, pp. 8 and 13.

41. *Report on e-Parliament Conference on Space Security*, September 14, 2005; 2105 Rayburn House Office Building, Washington, DC.

42. Theresa Hitchens, Center for Defense Information, "USAF Transformation Flight Plan Highlights Space Weapons," February 19, 2003; see also Leonard David, "U.S. Air Force Plans for Future War in Space," *Space.com*, February 22, 2004.

43. In addition to the projected initial cost of space-based systems, the cost of these weapons seems particularly prone to increases, and their schedules of development and deployment to delays. William Hartung reports that "even Space Power Caucus co-chair Wayne Allard (R-CO) felt compelled to lecture the Air Force and its contractors at a September 23, 2005 forum, stating that 'We in Congress are tired of the frequent cost increases and schedule delays. We have heard all the excuses and they are not good enough. In many respects, the Air Force and its contractors have lost all credibility with Congress when it comes to space acquisition programs.'" William D. Hartung with Frida Berrigan, Michelle Ciarrocca, and Jonathan Wingo, "Tangled Web 2005: A Profile of the Missile Defense and Space Weapons Lobbies," World Policy Institute, www.worldpolicy.org/projects/arms/reports/tangledweb.html.

44. The Pew Research Center for the People and the Press, December 5, 2005. See featured survey, "'U.S. Should Mind Its Own Business' Internationally," and "U.S. Image Up Slightly, but Still Negative," June 23, 2005, info@people-pres.org.

45. James Oberg, *Toward a Theory of Space Power* (GPO, 1999), pp. 15–16.

46. Michael Moore, "Full Spectrum Dominance" Conference, Airlie House, May 16–17, 2005.

47. *Report on e-Parliament Conference on Space Security*, September 14, 2004; 2105 Rayburn House Office Building, Washington, DC.

48. *Space Security 2003* (The Eisenhower Institute, 2004), p. 36.

49. Graham tells the story of how on January 25, 1995, the Russians picked up a rocket launch from Norway. The Russians feared it was a possible attack against Moscow, although in fact it was an atmospheric sounding rocket conducting scientific observations, and the Russians had been notified of the launch several weeks earlier. Only two minutes before the deadline to order nuclear retaliation, the Russians realized their mistake and called off their strategic strike. Thomas Graham Jr., "Space Weapons and the Risk of Accidental Nuclear War," *Arms Control Today*, Arms Control Association, December 2005. Despite such incidents, little work has been done to stop the risk of accidental nuclear war. Eric Rosenberg of *The Hearst Newspapers* reports on April 9, 2006, "Nearly six years after the U.S. and Russia agreed to build a joint military center in Moscow to reduce the risk of accidental nuclear war, work on the project has stalled because the two nations can't agree about taxes and legal liability. The project announced by President Clinton and Russian President Vladimir Putin in June 2000 was to be completed in 2002. But aside from identifying the site and setting up some communications cables, no work has been done to make the center a reality."

50. Everett Dolman, "Space Weapons and U.S. Military Transportation," "Full Spectrum Dominance" Conference, Airlie House, May 16–17, 2005.

51. Tim Weiner, "Air Force Seeks Bush's Approval for Space Weapons Programs," *New York Times*, May 18, 2005.

52. William J. Broad, of the *New York Times*, reported on April 2, 2006, the possibility of a major fraud in missile defense contracting. He writes, "A senior Congressional investigator has accused his agency of covering up a scientific fraud among builders of a $26 billion system meant to shield the nation from nuclear attack. . . . The investigator, Subrata Ghoshroy of the Government Accountability Office, led technical analyses of a prototype warhead for the anti-missile weapon in an 18-month study, winning awards for his 'great care' and 'tremendous skill and patience.' Mr. Ghoshroy now says his agency ignored evidence that the two main contractors had doctored data, skewed test results, and made false statements in a 2002 report that credited the contractors with revealing the warhead's failings to the government." The main contractor was Boeing.

53. *Report on e-Parliament Conference on Space Security*, September 14, 2005; 2105 Rayburn House Office Building, Washington, DC.

54. Bryan Bender of the *Boston Globe* reports on March 14, 2006, "Specialists believe the classified portion of the $439 [Defense] budget, blacked out for national security reasons, almost certainly includes other space-related programs."

55. *Space Security 2003* (The Eisenhower Institute, 2004), p. 8.

56. See Theresa Hitchens, "Ballistic Missile Defense System's Draft Programmatic Environmental Impact Statement: Missile Defense Agency Fails to Adequately Address Dangers of Orbital Debris to Objects and People in Space, in the Air and on the Ground," October 18, 2004. See also her "Weapons in Space: Silver Bullet or Russian Roulette? The Policy Implications of U.S. Pursuit of Space-Based Weapons," April 18, 2002. Hitchens' writings on the problem of outer space debris are definitive.

57. Simon Collard-Wexler, Jessy Cowan-Sharp, Sarah Estabrooks, Ambassador Thomas Graham Jr., Dr. Robert Lawson, and Dr. William Marshall, *Space Security 2004* (Northview Press), p. 9.

58. Theresa Hitchens, *Future Security in Space: Charting a Cooperative Course*, Center for Defense Information, Washington, DC, September 2004, pp. 37–40; the citation of Admiral Ellis is from Warren Ferster, "Military Bandwidth Demand Energizes Market," *Space News*, August 25, 2003.

59. Simon Collard-Wexler, Jessy Cowan-Sharp, Sarah Estabrooks, Ambassador Thomas Graham Jr., Dr. Robert Lawson, and Dr. William Marshall, *Space Security 2004* (Northview Press), p. xv.

60. *Space Security 2006,* mailto:sestabrooks@plowshares.ca. Also, see the directory of satellites maintained by the Union of Concerned Scientists. The number of military satellites is approximate because many satellites have dual military and civilian purposes.

61. Simon Collard-Wexler, Jessy Cowan-Sharp, Sarah Estabrooks, Ambassador Thomas Graham Jr., Dr. Robert Lawson, and Dr. William Marshall, *Space Security 2004* (Northview Press), pp. xv and 87–98; see also *Europe in Space,* Centre for European Reform, October 2004. *The Japan Times* reports, "In a shift away from a nearly 40-year-old commitment to an exclusively nonmilitary space program, the ruling Liberal Democratic Party announced plans Tuesday to draft a bill that would authorize Japan's military to use space for self-defense. The bill, which would reverse the current policy limiting space to civilian purposes, will allow the Defense Agency to build and operate high-resolution reconnaissance satellites." "Bill in works to officially allow military use of space," *The Japan Times,* http://search.japantimes.co.jp/print/mn2006329al.html.

62. *Report on e-Parliament Conference on Space Security,* September 14, 2004; 2105 Rayburn House Office Building, Washington, DC.

63. Daniel Keohane, Introduction, *Europe in Space,* Centre for European Reform, October 2004. As reported by Xavier Pasco in the same publication, "European countries already possess some space-based military assets. These programmes cover two main areas: earth observation and telecommunications. Only France has its own spy satellites, although Germany is developing its own system. The UK has privileged access to imagery from U.S. spy satellites, which makes the British reluctance to develop a system for satellite photography understandable. And France, Italy, Spain, and the UK all have some telecommunications assets."

64. "Weaponization of Space Will Have Unpredictable Consequences," Andrei Kislyakov, Political Commentator for *RIA Novosti,* Moscow, April 7, 2006.

5. Alternatives to Weapons in Outer Space

1. Melody by Don Swader, lyrics by June Hershey, 1941.

2. U.S. Air Force Advisory Board, "New World Vistas: Air and Space Power for the 21st Century," *Space Technology,* 1996.

3. This disdain for treaties is also shown in the personnel policies of the Bush administration. Warren P. Strobel of the *Knight Ridder Newspapers* reported on February 7, 2006, "State Department officials appointed by President Bush have sidelined key career weapons experts and replaced them with less experienced political operatives who share the White House and Pentagon's distrust of international negotiations and treaties."

4. See Michael Klare, *Resource Wars: The New Landscape of Global Conflict* (Henry Holt, 2001), and *Blood and Oil: The Dangers and Consequences of America's Growing Dependency on Imported Petroleum* (Metropolitan Books, 2004); Paul Roberts, *The End of Oil: On the Edge of a Perilous New World* (Houghton Mifflin, 2004). See also Edward O. Wilson, *The Future of Life* (Vintage Books, 2002).

5. Jeffrey D. Sachs, *The End of Poverty: Economic Possibilities for Our Time* (The Penguin Press, 2005).

6. See testimony of Nicholas Dunlop, Secretary-General of the e-Parliament, *Report on e-Parliament Conference on Space Security*, September 14, 2004; 2105 Rayburn House Office Building, Washington, DC.

7. "International Security in Outer Space Critical, Fragile and Rapidly Evolving: Space Security 2006 Report Released Today," sestabrooks@plowshares.ca.

8. Theresa Hitchens, *Future Security in Space: Charting a Cooperative Course*, Center for Defense Information, September 2004, pp. 8–11, and 44; see also her "Engaging the Reluctant Superpower: Practical Measures of Ensuring Space Security," Center for Defense Information, April 1, 2005.

9. Charles D. Ferguson and Dinshaw Mistry, "Moving Away from Missile Programs," *Boston Globe*, June 19, 2006.

10. The Henry L. Stimson Center, Model Code of Conduct for the Prevention of Incidents and Dangerous Military Practices in Outer Space, http://www.stimson .org/wos/pdf/codeofconduct.pdf.

11. As Theresa Hitchens points out, the 1989 Prevention of Dangerous Military Activities Agreement between the United States and the Soviet Union and the 1982 UN Convention on the Law of the Sea provide useful precedents for an international agreement on outer space. *Future Security in Space: Charting a Cooperative Course*, Center for Defense Information, September 2004, pp. 84 and 86.

12. Michael Krepon with Christopher Clary, *Space Assurance or Space Dominance? The Case Against Weaponizing Space*, pp. 115–116 (The Henry L. Stimson Center, 2003).

13. The United States also needs to resist supporting treaties that are not meaningful. The Strategic Offensive Reductions Treaty, called the "Moscow Treaty," calls for the reduction of nuclear warheads to a level of 1,700 to 2,200 by December 31, 2012, but it does not demand that the weapons be destroyed; it has no schedule, no verification procedures, and can be easily abrogated. The current Fissile Material Cut-off Treaty offered by the United States has no verification procedures.

14. With the election of Prime Minister Stephen Harper, the Canadian position not to participate in ballistic missile defense may change, particularly in view of

the appointment of Derek Burney, a strong supporter of BMD, to the transition team.

15. Judith Ingram, "Putin Urges Weapons-Treaty Talks with U.S.," *Associated Press*, June 27, 2006.

16. All three foreign speakers at the "Full Spectrum Dominance" Conference, Dr. Polanyi, Dr. Yermakov, and Dr. Zhang, pronounced positions which have been confirmed by their governments.

17. The 2006 report of the National Air and Space Intelligence Center states that "the number of warheads of Chinese ICBMs capable of threatening the United States is expected to grow to *well over 100 in the next 15 years*," www.nukestrat.com/us/afn/threats.htm.

18. Simon Collard-Wexler, Jessy Cowan-Sharp, Sarah Estabrooks, Ambassador Thomas Graham Jr., Dr. Robert Lawson, and Dr. William Marshall, *Space Security 2004* (Northview Press), p. 25.

19. Michael Krepon with Christopher Clary, *Space Assurance or Space Dominance? The Case Against Weaponizing Space* (The Henry L. Stimson Center, 2003), pp. 91–101; see particularly pp. 98–99.

20. A problem that would have to be worked out is how to include the increasing number of private or commercial launchers in an "international" treaty.

21. This was a joint working paper called "Possible Elements for a Future International Legal Agreement on the Prevention of Deployment of Weapons in Outer Space."

22. Michael Krepon with Christopher Clary, *Space Assurance or Space Dominance? The Case Against Weaponizing Space* (The Henry L. Stimson Center, 2003), p. 110.

23. Stephanie Nebehay, "U.S. Insists on Right to Develop Arms for Outer Space," *Reuters*, June 13, 2006.

24. Peter Slevin, *Washington Post*, April 17, 2004.

25. *Airpower Journal*, Winter 1998, p. 46.

26. Nancy Gallagher, "The Peaceful Uses of Outer Space (1957–2005): Environmental and Weather Observation, Communications, Arms Control, and Global Economics," "Full Spectrum Dominance" Conference, Airlie House, May 16–17, 2005.

27. Theresa Hitchens, *Future Security in Space: Charting a Cooperative Course*, Center for Defense Information, Washington, DC, September 2004, p. 25.

28. Statement by John R. Bolton to the Conference on Disarmament, Geneva, January 24, 2002.

29. Theresa Hitchens, *Future Security in Space*, p. 69. See "Annual Report on the Military Power of the People's Republic of China," FY04 Report to the

Congress on PRC Military Power Pursuant to the FY2000 National Defense Authorization Act, May 29, 2004, p. 6 and pp. 41–42.

30. *New York Times*, October 12, 2005, p. A9.

31. See Phillip C. Sanders, "China's Future in Space: Implications for U.S. Security," *adAstra, the Magazine of the National Space Society*, http://www.space.com/adastra/china_implications_0505/html.

32. "Drawing the Line: The Path to Controlling Weapons in Space," *Disarmament Diplomacy*, no. 66 (September 2002), p. 5.

33. The latest version is the Space Preservation Act of 2005 (H.R. 2420), sponsored by Rep. Kucinich, and co-sponsored by 34 members of Congress.

34. Carol Rosin and Alfred Webre, "How to Proceed with the Space Weaponization Treaty," International Network of Engineers and Scientists Against Proliferation, *Bulletin 20—Proposals for a Space Weaponization Ban*, http://www.inesap.org/bulletin20bul20art17.htm; see also "Legislation and World Treaty Banning Space-Based Weapons to be Signed in 2002," Institute for Cooperation in Space, Position Paper, November 29, 2001.

35. There was also massive international public support for the Land Mine Treaty inspired by Princess Diana.

36. "Full Spectrum Dominance" Conference, Airlie House, May 16–17, 2005. See also Bruce Gagnon, *Come Together Right Now: Organizing Stories from a Fading Empire* (Just Write Books, 2005).

Appendix 1

1. This section is based in part on the presentation of David Wright, Co-Director and Senior Scientist, Global Security Program, Union of Concerned Scientists & Research Scientists, Security Studies Program, MIT, at the "Full Spectrum Dominance" Conference at Airlie House, May 16–17, 2005; see also Michael Krepon with Christopher Clary, *Space Assurance or Space Dominance? The Case Against Weaponizing Space* (The Henry L. Stimson Center, 2003), pp. 63–64, and *Space Security 2003* (The Eisenhower Institute, 2004); and David Wright, Laura Grego, and Lisbeth Gronlund, *The Physics of Space Security*, American Academy of Arts and Sciences, 2005. This appendix also draws upon an inventory of world satellites prepared in January 2006 by the Union of Concerned Scientists.

Index

The letter *n* following a page number indicates a note on that page.